The Persistent Poverty of African Americans in the United States

The Persistent Poverty of African Americans in the United States

The Impact of Public Policy

Daphne M. Cooper

ANTHEM PRESS

Anthem Press
An imprint of Wimbledon Publishing Company
www.anthempress.com

This edition first published in UK and USA 2025
by ANTHEM PRESS
75–76 Blackfriars Road, London SE1 8HA, UK
or PO Box 9779, London SW19 7ZG, UK
and
244 Madison Ave #116, New York, NY 10016, USA

British Library Cataloguing-in-Publication Data
A catalogue record for this book is available from the British Library.

Library of Congress Cataloging-in-Publication Data: 2024937522
A catalog record for this book has been requested.

ISBN-13: 978-1-83999-188-2 (pbk)
ISBN-10: 1-83999-188-7 (pbk)

This title is also available as an e-book.

CONTENTS

FOREWORD

Dr. Daphne Cooper

My first encounter with Daphne Cooper was in 2007. She was enrolled as a graduate student in the Department of Political Science at Clark Atlanta University, where I served as a professor. Dr. Cooper enrolled in several of my classes during her matriculation in the department. Among the classes was a seminar course organized around poverty policies in the United States. The question of the persistence of poverty among certain groups was the question that stood out for Dr. Cooper. She wanted to determine if there existed a link between poverty and public policies. Specifically, those policies which have as their goal the elimination of poverty.

While a student in my courses, Dr. Cooper and I collaborated on research projects. These collaborations were centered around inequality and public policies. In pursuit of her doctoral degree, Dr. Cooper conducted extensive research on the persistence of poverty among certain classes in the United States. She discovered that the answer to persistent poverty was as much a structural problem as it was an individual failing.

I served as chair of Dr. Cooper's dissertation committee, which gave me insight into her research process. However, more importantly, I was able to see how dedicated Dr. Cooper is to discover the why of a question and issue. This is evident in this book. The book is an expansion of the research she began as a doctoral student. This book digs deeper into the why of the persistence of poverty.

Dr. Cooper has used her extensive research in this area to explore the reasons for the vast and increasing inequality among groups in the United States. Dr. Cooper demonstrates that a society that is founded on individualism will not enact policies that challenge the status quo. Dr. Cooper argues that policies grounded in individualism and minimalism will produce short-term policies that must show immediate results.

Dr. Cooper challenges many of the notions on why poverty persists among very identifiable groups in U.S. society. Old notions are undermined and reasons as to why we should reconsider policymaking are thoroughly examined.

William Boone, PhD
Professor Emeritus
Department of Political Science
Clark Atlanta University

INTRODUCTION

The significance of this scholarship is to investigate how and why African Americans in the United States remain in persistent poverty. This research is important because it addresses the harsh inequalities that exist among African Americans through the use of federal policies. This scholarship challenges the United States' governmental systems and its incorrect, misdirected policies that were created to minimize or eliminate poverty. It pleads with policymakers to reconceptualize poverty, moving them away from the improper, fixed, preconceived notions, and unfavorable ideologies about the poor. This scholarship is instrumental because it offers a prevailing paradigm shift in the United States' public policy. It provides the federal government policymakers with prescriptions for the future that will look at problems differently, focusing on the structures within the governmental system instead of blaming the powerless individual. The goal is to promote new policy initiatives and recommendations for the future, with the use of specific guidelines for policymakers to incorporate.

Policymakers will utilize this research to gain new knowledge and information, as well as implement new public policies that would better address the poor and underprivileged in the United States. This information is useful to policymakers, allowing them to improve the quality of life among those individuals and families that remain persistently poor, by allocating more resources and funding and distributing it equally. This information will raise the public's awareness about the "who is" the face of poverty and how it exists in a wealthy country, like the United States. This book will provide everyone with an understanding about the federal policies that were created to lessen or eliminate poverty, but actually perpetuated poverty among specific minority groups. This study demonstrates how the federal government uses its power through the creation of policies such as public housing, residential racial segregation, welfare, and underfunded educational systems. It will raise the public's awareness about the government's power and policies, which may encourage citizens to become more involved in the political process once they understand how it will or have directly affected their lives.

This scholarship contributes to the field of political science, sociology, public policy, and public administration. It is intended to encourage other scholars and policymakers to pursue further research on poverty and race. Public officials and community organizers may become interested in this research because it will provide a thorough structural critique of the United States' public policies for the poor.

Organization of the Book

The book consists of five chapters. Chapter 1 includes the Introduction, The Problem, Theoretical Framework, Definition of the Terms, Research Questions, and Methodology; Chapter 2 will provide a review of selected literature; Chapter 3 outlines the History and Responses to Poverty in the United States—Case Study War on Poverty Anti-poverty Programs; Chapter 4 will represent findings; Chapter 5 will summarize the research and discuss its conclusions and implications.

Chapter 1

POVERTY MEANS DIFFERENT THINGS TO DIFFERENT PEOPLE WHAT IS POVERTY?

Poverty is hunger. Poverty is a lack of shelter. Poverty is being sick and not being able to see a doctor. Poverty reflects not single causes but cumulative disadvantages, and disadvantages do not cascade by accident.[1] Persistent poverty can be seen among people who experience deprivation over many years and whose average incomes are below the poverty line for an extended period of time; it is those who are experiencing hardship because of their stage in the life cycle; and those who are discriminated against because of their social position at the local, regional, or national level.[2] Individuals who live in persistent poverty experience several forms of disadvantage and are the least likely to benefit from public policy, which will keep them in poverty and block off their opportunities to escape.[3]

African Americans in the United States are disproportionately impacted by poverty than any other population group. According to the United States Census Bureau, between 2021 and 2022, the poverty rate increased for non-Hispanic Whites (from 8.1 percent to 8.6 percent), for African Americans (from 19.5 percent to 17.1 percent), and for Hispanics (from 17.1 percent to 16.5 percent). For Asians, the 2022 poverty rate (8.6 percent) was not statistically different from the 2021 poverty rate.[4]

---

1 Ann Chih Lin and David R. Harris, "Why is American Poverty Still Colored in the Twenty-First Century?" In *The Colors of Poverty: Why Racial and Ethnic Disparities Persist.* Edited by Ann Chih Lin and David R. Harris (New York, NY: Russell Sage Foundation, 2008), 4.

2 David Hulme, Karen Moore, and Andrew Shepherd, "Chronic Poverty: Meanings and Analytical Frameworks" (2001). www.chronicpoverty.org.

3 Ibid.

4 United States Census Bureau. http://www.census.gov/hhes/www/poverty (Accessed December 19, 2023).

History has shown that substantial progress for African Americans has occurred over the last 40 years, but the life chances of the average African American or Latino child today are still very different from those of the average White or Asian child.[5] According to Lin and Harris, times have changed in the United States, but what has not changed is the use of race, which creates categories that guide the distribution of opportunities as well as vulnerabilities toward negative treatment.

Ann Chih Lin and David R. Harris argue that race is at the center of any attempt to assess poverty because in the United States, our economy, our cultural frameworks, our repertoires, and our governmental policies have been shaped by a history of racial relations and racially influenced decision-making. As a result, our institutions, practices, and beliefs can foster racial discrimination disadvantage without any deliberate effort to discriminate. However, it is extremely important to consider the significance of discrimination in the context of persistent poverty among members of racial or ethnic minority groups.[6]

The primary purpose of this book is to introduce and question the persistent poverty that exists among African Americans in the United States. The significance of researching persistent poverty among African Americans is that it will provide undergraduate/graduate students, scholars, sociologists, and policymakers with information to understand what constitutes poverty, how and why African Americans have remained poor and underprivileged in the United States. This book will provide information that will be useful in improving public policies that are related to the lives and social conditions of African Americans. This book focuses on factors that influence American governmental policies and how these factors effect policies concerned with African Americans. Lyndon B. Johnson's War on Poverty policies serve as a case study of U.S. policy. I have analyzed the Great Society programs and policies that were created to eliminate or lessen poverty, which include the Public Housing Act of 1964 and Housing and Urban Development Act of 1965, education, and former president Bill Clinton's Temporary Assistance to Needy Families Act of 1996 (TANF). This book has analyzed the attitudes and behaviors of African Americans who have been poor over a long period of time from past longitudinal studies.

5 Lin and Harris, "Why is American Poverty Still Colored in the Twenty-First Century?" 4.

6 Devah Pager, "The Dynamics of Discrimination." In *The Colors of Poverty: Why Racial and Ethnic Disparities Persist.* Edited by Ann Chih Lin and David R. Harris (New York, NY: Russell Sage Foundation, 2008), 2.

Historical Background

This book utilizes President Lyndon B. Johnson's unconditional War on Poverty Great Society Legislation as a case study because, for the first time, the United States government was given the power to intervene directly to ensure recognition of the constitutional rights of all its citizens in every state.[7] Most importantly, the War on Poverty was the United States government's systematic approach used to eliminate or minimize poverty. The legislation targeted African Americans for inclusion on the agenda, which represented a turning point in United States social policy.

Although the War on Poverty did not eradicate poverty in the United States, it was selected as a case study because it had a profound effect on many people's lives and it significantly shaped the social and economic commitments of the federal government toward African Americans: it was the most important piece of legislation concerning equal opportunity; it was the main effort used to eliminate discrimination throughout American society, which gave a guarantee to people of color, an equal opportunity.[8] Remarkably, many of the War on Poverty programs established during the 1960s are still in existence today such as medical insurance; the food stamp program; the extension of minimum wage laws; federal aid to education; the construction of libraries, hospitals, and nursing homes; mass transit; and urban renewal projects.[9] In this scholarship, the War on Poverty policies were examined and a policy analysis was performed that determined the effects of each policy and its influence on African Americans.

The War on Poverty was an ambitious governmental effort used to address the problem of persistent poverty in the United States; it was complex in its origins, its implementation, and its impact. Its programs and philosophies were born out of the political discomfort caused by the persistence of poverty after World War II. Therefore, the difficult questions of citizenship, civil rights and social reform in the United States had to be addressed. The administrations of President John F. Kennedy and his successor Lyndon B. Johnson became the primary organizers to give a governmental response to the poverty crisis. They had to deal with the concern that poverty would threaten America's progress, and both administrations pushed for economic growth that would create full employment, and social reform that would enable the

7 Linda Faye Williams, *The Constraint of Race: Legacies of White Skin Privilege in America* (University Park, PA: The Pennsylvania State University Press, 2003), 125.

8 Ibid.

9 Michael L. Gillette, *Launching The War On Poverty: An Oral History* (New York, NY: Twayne Publishers, 1996), 9.

poor to access what President Johnson called "the good life." Lyndon Johnson wanted presidential power so that he could give things to people, to all sorts of people, especially to the poor and blacks.[10]

The Great Society legislation benefited African Americans, unlike the New Deal programs that failed to address the status of African Americans in any fundamental way. In contrast to Lyndon B. Johnson, Franklin Delano Roosevelt and Kennedy had no plans to sacrifice their domestic and economic programs on the stage of civil rights. Kennedy produced limited benefits for the poor and his efforts against poverty were piecemeal, hesitating, and limited to implementing safe policy.[11]

Lyndon B. Johnson recognized that blacks and Latinos suffered from the lack of access to quality health programs, decent housing, and jobs. He initiated legislation to rectify these inequities by transforming the nation's social policy. He declared an unconditional War on Poverty to create a new institutional base for antipoverty policies and civil rights actions, of which many African Americans were beneficiaries of through the effects of economic opportunities. Lyndon Johnson's goal was to help individuals, families, and communities to help themselves.

The Johnson administration pushed through an unprecedented amount of antipoverty legislation, such as The Economic Opportunity Act of 1964, which provided the basis for the Office of Economic Opportunity (OEO), the Job Corps, Volunteers in Service to America (VISTA), Upward Bound, Head Start, Legal Services, the Neighborhood Youth Corps, the Community Action Program (CAP), the College Work-Study program, Neighborhood Development Centers, small business loan programs, rural programs, migrant worker programs, remedial education projects, and local health care centers.[12]

The antipoverty effort, however, did not stop there; it encompassed a range of Great Society legislation far broader than the Economic Opportunity Act alone. Other important measures with antipoverty functions included the Revenue Act of 1964, the Civil Rights Act of 1964, the Food Stamp Act of 1964, the Elementary and Secondary Education Act of 1965, the Higher Education Act of 1965, the Social Security amendments creating Medicare/Medicaid (1965), the creation of the Department of Housing and Urban

10 Quoted in Doris Kearns, *Lyndon Johnson and the American Dream* (New York, NY: Harper & Row, 1976), 53–54.

11 Kenneth O'Neil, *Nixon's Piano: Presidents and Racial Politics From Washington to Clinton* (New York, NY: Free Press, 1995).

12 Gillette, *Launching The War On Poverty*, 9.

Development (1965), the Voting Rights Act of 1965, the Model Cities Act of 1966, the Fair Housing Act of 1968, several job-training programs, and various Urban Renewal-related projects.[13]

The War on Poverty constituted a new conceptual approach to the problem of poverty. It was an attempt to uncover and strike at the roots of poverty, to destroy its causes, instead of treating its symptoms. The War on Poverty was not concerned with helping the poor to become more comfortable in their poverty, but rather, with helping the poor to rise out of poverty.[14] According to Daniel Halloran, the antipoverty programs were rushed through Congress on the tide of emotionalism following President Kennedy's death. The War on Poverty was not a product of a long, fruitful period of congressional debate. It did not constitute a well-structured administrative plan; it was viewed as a disjointed series of programs clustered around a dynamic new concept that society should attack the causes of poverty instead of treating its symptoms.[15] According to Halloran, the War on Poverty was unsuccessful because of the inadequate administrative direction at the highest levels, the failure to obtain broad support, and the antipoverty programs never received the degree of financial support necessary to intensify the seriousness against the causes of poverty because of the fiscal pressure from Southeast Asia.

One of the chief reasons for the failure of the antipoverty programs was its unfortunate involvement in the liberal-conservative ideological confrontation in American political society. Conservative attitudes toward poverty, welfare, and the antipoverty programs have shown a considerable variety of opinions ranging from the refusal to admit that the United States has a poverty problem and a return to Adam Smith's economic concept that any government action to relieve poverty will only serve to disrupt the self-regulating nature of economic society.[16] Some conservatives criticize public welfare as a waste of their hard-earned tax money and having no lasting benefit to the poor.

The Problem

American politics and power have disadvantaged African Americans through federal policies, causing them to remain poor and underprivileged in the United States. History demonstrates that African Americans have inherited

13 Ibid.

14 Daniel F. Halloran, "Progress Against Poverty: The Governmental Approach." *Public Administration Review* 28, no. 3 (May–June 1968): 209.

15 Ibid.

16 Ibid., 210.

gateless poverty: exacerbated by living without training and skills; living in slums without decent medical care; having the devastating heritage of the long years of slavery; and a century of oppression, hatred, and injustice.[17] African Americans in the United States started off at a disadvantage; they were hobbled by chains for years and then abruptly liberated, and brought to the starting line expecting to compete with all of the others.[18] The Civil Rights policies attempted to address the fundamental inequalities between whites and blacks by dramatically changing their conditions. However, Civil Rights policies did not address the ways in which race was embedded in American law and society through institutions and outcomes such as residential racial segregation; the criminal justice system; or the comparatively higher poverty rates that many African Americans faced. The Civil Rights victories of the 1960s failed to address the policy-making process and a set of preferences that, though not race-specific, had racial impacts.

Daniel R. Meyer and Geoffrey Wallace in "Poverty Levels and Trends in Comparative Perspectives," argued that there were substantial differences in poverty rates that have persisted since 1968. The highest poverty rates that have been above 20 percent include African Americans, people living in a family whose head of household does not have a job, a high school diploma, or a college degree. In the United States, those with low earnings or no earnings were at a very high risk of poverty because the social programs that supplement low earnings are generally not generous enough to lessen or eliminate poverty. These characteristics highlight the critical importance of the labor market and the fact that African Americans have higher poverty rates because race is still strongly connected to opportunity and outcome in the United States.[19]

African Americans are many times more likely to be long-term poor than whites are, and they are much less likely to be upwardly mobile, either within or across generations.[20] Research shows that there is a dramatic difference in

---

17 Lyndon B. Johnson, "To Fulfill These Rights: Commencement Address at Howard University, June 4, 1965." In *Public Papers of the Presidents of the United States: Lyndon B. Johnson, 1965.* Volume II (Washington, DC: Government Printing Office).

18 Ibid.

19 Daniel R. Meyer and Geoffrey L. Wallace, "Poverty Levels and Trends in Comparative Perspectives." In *Changing Poverty, Changing Policies.* Edited by Maria Cancian and Sheldon Danziger (New York, NY: Russell Sage Foundation, 2009), 56–57.

20 Mary Corcoran, "Mobility, Persistence, and the Consequences of Poverty for Children: Child and Adult Outcomes." In *Understanding Poverty.* Edited by Sheldon H. Danziger and Robert H. Haveman (New York, NY: Russell Sage Foundation, 2001), 128.

poverty rates across different racial categories. In 2005, a quarter of all African Americans lived below the poverty line compared to only a tenth of whites. The poverty rates for all persons make considerable variation between racial and ethnic subgroups. Poverty rates for African Americans and Hispanics greatly exceed the national average. Poverty rates in 2007 were statistically unchanged for non-Hispanic Whites (8.2 percent), Blacks (24.5 percent), and Asians (10.2 percent) from 2006. The poverty rate increased for Hispanics (21.5 percent in 2007, up from 20.6 percent in 2006).[21] In 2008, 24.7 percent of African Americans and 23.2 percent of Hispanics were poor, compared to 8.6 percent of Whites, and 11.8 percent of Asians. According to the U.S. Census Bureau in 2009, 43.6 million people were in poverty, up from 39.8 million in 2008—the third consecutive annual increase in the number of people in poverty. Between 2008 and 2009, the poverty rate increased for non-Hispanic Whites (from 8.6 percent to 9.4 percent), for Blacks (from 24.7 percent to 25.8 percent), and for Hispanics (from 23.2 percent to 25.3 percent). For Asians, the 2009 poverty rate (12.5 percent) was not statistically different from the 2008 poverty rate.[22] Poverty rates are highest among families headed by single women, particularly if they are African American or Hispanic.[23] To date, the U.S. Census Bureau reported that between 2021 and 2022, the poverty rate increased for non-Hispanic Whites (from 8.1 percent to 8.6 percent), for African Americans a slight decrease (from 19.5 percent to 17.1 percent), and for Hispanics (from 17.1 percent to 16.5 percent) but still higher for longer periods of time. For Asians, the 2022 poverty rate (8.6 percent) was not statistically different from the 2021 poverty rate.[24] Poverty is an American class problem that disproportionately affects African Americans and Hispanic Americans at an alarming rate but also affects white Americans.

Ideologies have also perpetuated persistent poverty among African Americans through the use of governmental policies. There are two major ideologies in the United States that influence and guide the behavior of individuals and institutions, conservatism and liberalism. Both ideologies guide people, groups, and communities in selecting goals and choosing the means

21 Carmen DeNavas-Walt, Bernadette D. Proctor, and Jessica C. Smith, U.S. Census Bureau, Current Population Reports, "Income, Poverty, and Health Insurance Coverage in the United States: 2007" (Washington, DC: U.S. Government Printing Office, 2008), 60.

22 U.S. Census Bureau. http://www.census.gov/hhes/www/poverty/about/overview/index.html.

23 U.S. Bureau of Census, 2008 Report.

24 United States Census Bureau. http://www.census.gov/hhes/www/poverty (Accessed December 19, 2023).

to achieve them. Conservatism is a set of beliefs that include a limited role for the government in helping individuals; support for traditional values; believing that the individual is responsible for his or her own well-being; and opposing government programs that redistribute income or change the status of individuals.[25] Liberalism is a set of beliefs that include advocacy of government action to improve the welfare of individuals; support for civil rights; and tolerance for political and social change. Liberals believe that the government should take positive action to reduce poverty, redistribute income from wealthier classes to poorer ones, and regulate the economy.[26] Liberals are often seen as an influential force within the Democratic Party, and conservatives are often regarded as the most influential in the Republican Party.

The persistent poverty that exists among African Americans is a result of the unanticipated consequence of public policy that was intended to alleviate social problems but has, in fact, caused them to worsen. There has been considerable debate in both academic and policy arenas over the extent of long-term poverty. Some scholars argue that there is no long-term poverty problem and that most poverty is temporary and reflects short-run adjustment problems or life-cycle changes. Other scholars argue that some individuals and families remain poor for longer periods, perhaps over generations. One view blames poverty persistence on poor labor market opportunities, segregation, discrimination, inadequate under-funded schools, and the lack of community resources in disadvantaged neighborhoods. An additional group points to the work and marriage disincentives in the welfare system; the increasing number of female-headed households; the increases in teen pregnancy and illegitimacy; deviant subcultures and the personal deficiencies of the poor.

According to the Institute for Research on Poverty, African Americans and Hispanics have poverty rates that greatly exceed the national average. Poverty levels differ depending on where people live; the metropolitan poverty rate differs greatly between suburbs and the central city; it also varies by region and within regions and in 2008 poverty was greater in the south.[27] According to Scott Allard, African Americans are impacted by federal housing policies, public housing practices, discriminatory mortgage lending, and racial steering, which played a major role in the creation of poor black neighborhoods. Douglas S. Massey argues that residential segregation is the

25 Barbara A. Bardes, Mack C. Shelley II, and Steffen W. Schmidt, *American Government and Politics Today: The Essentials* (Boston, MA: Wadsworth Cengage Learning, 2010), 18.

26 Ibid.

27 Douglas S. Massey and Nancy Denton, *American Apartheid: Segregation and the Making of the Underclass* (Cambridge, MA: Harvard University Press, 1993).

primary structural cause of the geographical concentration of poverty in the United States' urban areas. Research indicates that residential segregation is the principal structural feature of American society that's responsible for the perpetuation of poverty, which represents the primary cause of racial inequality in the United States.[28] According to Wilson, Massey, and Denton, racially segregated urban poverty is one of the most recognizable products of housing discrimination and housing policy in America.

In 1990, roughly 17 percent of all blacks lived in high-poverty areas—census tracts where the poverty rate exceeded 40 percent and blacks comprised about 50 percent of high-poverty tracts.[29] According to Michael A. Stoll, by the year 2000, 27 percent of blacks in central city areas lived below the poverty level and continue to make up the vast majority of the urban poor. Federal housing policies during the postwar era subsidized public housing developments for low-income households. Many large-scale public housing developments that were built during the twentieth century concentrated and isolated poor families, often minorities, into deteriorating buildings located in unsafe neighborhoods that were far from labor market opportunities.[30] Today, many of the government's programs and policies continue to perpetuate segregation and the concentration of poverty in African American communities, without the explicit design of earlier programs. For example, family public housing is highly segregated and predominantly located in areas of concentrated poverty. Similarly, since 2001, the federal government has implemented policy changes and budget cuts that have restricted affordable housing choice and mobility for participants in the Section 8 Housing Choice Voucher Program.[31] In addition, the Low-Income Housing Tax Credit provides an incentive to developers to develop affordable housing primarily in poor and predominantly minority neighborhoods, which often perpetuates residential segregation. These federal programs are augmented by the state and local government policies that contribute to residential segregation, including exclusionary zoning rules and school attendance boundaries.[32]

---

28 Ibid.

29 Paul Jargowsky, *Poverty and Place: Ghettos, Barrios, and the American City* (New York, NY: Russell Sage Foundation, 1997).

30 Alexander Von Hoffman, "High Ambitions: The Past and Future of American Low-Income Housing Policy." *Housing Policy Debate* 7, no. 3 (1996): 423–426.

31 Michael B. de Leeuw, Megan K. Whyte, Dale Ho, Catherine Meza, and Alexis Karteron, "Residential Segregation and Housing Discrimination in the United States: Violations of the International Convention on the Elimination of All Forms of Racial Discrimination." Executive Summary (December 2007).

32 Ibid., ii.

Public Housing policies have contributed significantly to the establishment and entrenchment of residential segregation and concentrated poverty throughout the United States. Most public housing built from the 1950s to 1970s was comprised of large, densely populated "projects," often consisting of high-rise buildings located in poor, racially segregated communities.[33] The federal government and individual housing authorities played an active and deliberate role in concentrating poverty in racially segregated public housing. Many cities established separate public housing for African American and white residents, whether explicitly stated or not.[34] Housing authorities often yielded to public and political pressure not to locate public housing or its tenants in white neighborhoods.[35]

Poor African Americans don't have adequate access to social services. Research has shown that living in a neighborhood highly segregated by race diminishes one's access to social service agencies, which are an increasingly important part of the contemporary social safety net. Scott W. Allard argues that a poor person living in a predominantly black or Hispanic neighborhood will have access to roughly half as many services as a poor person living in a predominantly white neighborhood. Inadequate access to job training and adult education programs reinforce the poor quality of public schools in many low-income areas to further increase the barriers to self-sufficiency and economic advancement.[36] Poverty, inequality, and joblessness persist in highly segregated impoverished communities. However, the policy tools and safety net programs developed to alleviate social problems are not readily accessible to the populations that are most in need, particularly the poor minorities.[37]

Poverty and welfare recipients are inextricably linked. Government programs may help low-income citizens meet their basic daily needs through cash assistance programs such as Temporary Assistance to Needy Families or food stamps, but there is a continuing fear that welfare itself has negative effects, which creates economic dependency and perpetuates a cycle of poverty. Joe Soss and Sandy Schram argue that racial disparities in welfare reform lie within its implementation. In their research, they show that the

33 Rod Solomon, "Public Housing Reform And Voucher Success: Progress and Challenges." *Brookings Institute* 2 (2005). (Federal Policy 235).

34 *NAACP v. HUD*, 817 F.2d149, 151 (1st Cir.1987).

35 *Walker v. HUD*, 743 F Supp. 1289, 1294 (N.D. Tex. 1989); *Gautreaux v. Chicago Housing Authority*, 296 F. Supp. 907, 913–14 (N.D. Ill. 1969).

36 Scott W. Allard, "Place, Race, and Access to the Safety Net." In *The Colors of Poverty Why Racial and Ethnic Disparities Persist*. Edited by Ann Chih Lin and David R. Harris (New York, NY: Russell Sage Foundation, 2008), 252.

37 Ibid., 253.

states with the highest proportion of African Americans and Latinos are more likely to impose sanctions and choose more restrictive policies. States with more African Americans are also likely to devolve authority to counties and other local jurisdictions, increasing the probability that implementation will vary by geography. The end result is that local differences cumulate nationwide to a welfare regime in which the majority of white recipients experience the most generous welfare programs and the majority of African American recipients experience the most restrictive.

According to David Mead, reforms during the 1960s shifted public assistance from a program that excluded people of color to a system epitomized by the stereotypical African American welfare mom. To conservatives, welfare continues to be a problem because African Americans lack the appropriate "cultural values" to get themselves out of poverty.[38] However, for many social activists and liberal academics, high welfare rates and the middle-class backlash against welfare are the direct result of racism.[39] According to the President's Commission for a National Agenda during the 1980s, "Our welfare system continues to be a maze of uncoordinated programs that trap people into poverty and dependency." Additionally, in the State of Black America, 1980, Vernon Jordon writes about the need to replace the disastrous welfare system.[40] Poverty reduction was not among the stated purposes of the 1996 Welfare Reform Bill; the main goals were to reduce welfare dependency and encourage greater self-sufficiency, as well as to promote two-parent families as a context for having and raising children. Some welfare advocates argue that reducing poverty should be a specific component for the next phase of welfare reform.

The Questions

The following research questions were addressed to examine and determine which governmental policies perpetuated persistent poverty and/or contributed to a culture of poverty among African Americans in the United States. The following questions addressed the issues associated with persistent poverty in the United States.

---

38 Lawrence M. Mead, *The New Politics of Poverty: The Nonworking Poor in America* (New York, NY: HarperCollins Publishers, 1992),

39 Michael B. Katz, *The Undeserving Poor: From the War on Poverty to the War on Welfare* (New York, NY: Pantheon, 1989).

40 The Johnson Foundation, Box 567, Racine, WI. "Welfare Policy in the United States: A Critique and Some Proposals Derived from the Experience of Former Secretaries of Health, Education, and Welfare" (Document Resume, 1982), 6.

1. Are federal policies such as public housing and social welfare responsible for creating the persistent poverty that exists among African Americans in the United States?

This is an important question because the literature is mixed, as well as policymakers on the impact of public policies and the issue of poverty reduction. This book looks at federal policies in the areas of public housing, welfare, and education. The purpose of answering this question is for policymakers to have a positive outcome to create new policies that will better assist the poor. The answer to this question provides new knowledge and information about what constitutes poverty among specific groups and how to lessen or alleviate it. Better answers are needed because the same answers from over 42 years ago are still being utilized to address poverty.

Answering this question has given me the opportunity to examine American politics, race, and past policies that led to and created inadequate education, under-funded schools, deteriorating unsafe neighborhoods, and poor social conditions among African Americans. This question is intended to provide the readers with an understanding on how policy changes have affected African Americans, causing them to continuously lag behind white Americans.

2. Has a Culture of Poverty developed among African Americans and contributed to their persistent state of poverty? Does the Culture of Poverty exist? Has failed government policies created a Culture of Poverty?

This question was asked to determine if a culture of poverty exists, and if it's the reason why African Americans remain poor and underprivileged in the United States. Answering this question has helped to unravel the notion that once a culture of poverty comes into existence (meaning that both an adaption and a reaction of the poor to their marginal position in a class-stratified, highly individualistic, capitalist society), it tends to perpetuate itself from generation to generation, creating a lack of ambition, work ethic, and a sense of self-reliance. Answering this question is intended to disclose why specific groups exhibit certain behaviors. This question describes some of the reasons why African Americans remain poor and underprivileged in the United States. They include segregation, limited opportunities, and the external obstacles against advancement, which were determined by different historical circumstances. The answer to this question has led to further research, requesting a proper social analysis, that would lead to new policies that will better address the persistent poverty that exists among African Americans in the United States. Answering this question will inform policymakers/government institutions how they could become more effective and efficient when implementing poverty reduction policies. Incorporating new diversity and sensitivity training programs throughout governmental institutions will provide policymakers with a better understanding of the environments in which they serve. This question proves that policies will stimulate cultural responses or intensify cultural tensions.

Major Concepts and Theoretical Underpinnings

Mollie Orshansky developed the official definition of poverty in 1965 for the Social Security Administration. Poverty lines or family income needs were based on the cost of a nutritionally adequate diet for households of given size and composition, multiplied by three. According to the U.S. Census Bureau and the Office of Management and Budget's (OMB) Policy Directive 14, poverty is defined by a set of money income thresholds that vary by family size and composition to determine who is in poverty. If a family's total income is less than the family's threshold, then that family and every individual in that family is considered in poverty. The official poverty definition uses money income before taxes and does not include capital gains or non-cash benefits such as public housing, Medicaid, or food stamps.[41] In 2022, for a single person, the poverty line was $13,590 and for a family of three $23,030.

According to David Hulme, poverty is usually viewed as either a form of absolute or relative deprivation, but significant deprivation. Absolute poverty is perceived as subsistence below the minimum requirements for physical well-being, generally based on a quantitative proxy indicator, such as income or calories, but sometimes considering a broader package of goods and services. Alternatively, the relatively poor are those whose income or consumption level is below a particular fraction of the national average.[42] Poverty areas are defined as census tracts or block numbering areas (BNAs) where at least 20 percent of residents are below the poverty level. The poverty rate is defined as the percentage of people or families who are below the poverty level. People and families are classified as being in poverty if their income is less than their poverty threshold.

Persistent Poverty

Chronic or long-term poverty is defined as the percentage of people in poverty every month for the duration of a longitudinal survey panel, typically three

41 U.S. Census Bureau. http://www.unitedstatescensusbureau.com.

42 Hulme, Moore, and Shepherd, "Chronic Poverty."

to four years.[43] The U.S. Department of Agriculture's (USDA) Economic Research Service (ERS) defines 382 persistent poverty counties nationwide, in which at least 20 percent of the population are below the poverty threshold for three decades, as measured by four consecutive decennial censuses. In an article by David Hulme, Karen Moore, and Andrew Shepherd, titled "Chronic Poverty: Meanings and Analytical Frameworks," people who are chronically poor in terms of both duration and severity are those whose average incomes are well below the poverty line for an extended period of time; those experiencing deprivation because of their stage in the life cycle (older people, children, and widows); and those who are discriminated against because of their social position at the local, regional, or national level (marginalized castes, ethnic, racial or religious groups, refugees, Indigenous people, nomads and pastoralists, migrants).[44]

Public Policy

Public policy has been defined in many ways. Thomas Dye describes public policy as "what the government chooses to do, or not to do." Public policy is the outcome of struggle in government institutions over who gets what. B. Guy Peters defines public policy as the sum of government activities, whether pursued directly or indirectly through agents, as those activities that have an influence on the lives of citizens. According to Clark E. Cochran, the term public policy always refers to the actions of the government and the intentions that determine those actions. Making policy requires choosing among goals and alternatives, and choice always involves intention.[45] Policy is seldom a single action, but is most often a series of actions coordinated to achieve a goal.[46] Cochran defines public policy as an intentional course of action followed by a government institution or official for resolving an issue of public concern. According to Cochran, such a course of action must be manifested in laws, public statements, official regulations, or widely accepted and publicly visible patterns of behavior. Public policy is rooted in law and authority and coercion associated with the government.[47]

---

43 The Center For Rural Pennsylvania: A Legislative Agency of the Pennsylvania General Assembly. www.ruralpa.org.

44 Hulme, Moore, and Shepherd, "Chronic Poverty."

45 Clark E. Cochcran, Lawrence C. Meyer, T. R. Carr, and Joseph Cayer, *American Public Policy: An Introduction* (Boston, MA: Wadsworth Cengage Learning, 2009), 1.

46 Ibid.

47 Ibid. 2.

Public policy is concerned with the government's action or inaction to address a public issue. The government, whether it is city, state, or federal, develops public policy in terms of laws, regulations, decisions, and actions. According to Peters, there are three major parts of public policy that make real differences in the lives of citizens which include: Policy choices—the decisions made by politicians, civil servants, or others with authority to use public power to affect the lives of citizens; Policy outputs—policy choices being put into action; and Policy impacts—the effects that policy choices and policy outputs have on its citizens such as, making them wealthier, healthier, or the air they breathe less polluted.[48] These impacts may be influenced by other factors in the society such as, economic productivity, education, and economic programs, but they also reflect to some degree the failure of public policy choices and output.[49] According to Josen and Butler, policy-making is occasionally a dispassionate, systematic analysis and synthesis undertaken to identify, define, and address a public issue. More often, it is the "muddling through," which Charles Lindbolm calls "disjointed incrementalism." This is the "never ending process of successive steps in which continual nibbling is a substitute for a good bite."[50] Problems are never solved; instead, some analysis is done, a decision is made, unanticipated adverse consequences show up, more analysis is done and more decisions are made to remedy the adverse consequences and this goes on infinitely.[51] A public policy may not be a plan at all, it may be a decision to neither plan nor act, as recommended in Daniel Moynihan's "benign neglect."[52]

Michael Mintrom contends that public policy includes both empirical and normative investigation. He proposes that at the empirical level, there are issues of what the government does in practice and how this varies over time and between jurisdictions. At the normative level, key issues include what the governments ought to do and ought not do, and what principles should guide their decision-making; from this prescriptive, ethics lies at the heart

---

48 Guy B. Peters, *American Public Policy: Promise and Performance* (Washington, DC: CQ Press, 2007), 4.

49 Ibid., 5.

50 Charles Lindblom, *The Policy Making Process* (Englewood Cliffs, NJ: Prentice-Hall Review, 1968), 25.

51 K. A. Archibald, "Three Views of the Expert's Role in Policy Making: Systems Analysis, Incrementalism and the Clinical Approach." *Policy Sciences* 1 (1970).

52 Albert R. Josen and Lewis H. Butler, "Public Ethics and Policy Making." *The Hastings Report* 5, no. 4 (August 1975): 21.

of public policy, and is relevant.[53] Ethics refers to the standards of behavior on how human beings should act in many situations. Ethics is concerned with what is good and bad, right and wrong, just and unjust, or noble and ignoble.[54] Ethics can be useful to the policymaking process not in a theoretical relationship, but through the use of an ethical analysis in implementing policy.[55] In order for policymakers to make good ethical decisions, Thomas G. Plante suggests that they follow a framework for ethical decision-making which includes Integrity—strive to do the right thing in any given situation at all times; Competence—having knowledge and understanding of the issue; Responsibility—being accountable to others; Respect—show respect for others, acknowledge their humanity, dignity, and their right to be the people they are; and Concern—show concern for others, caring about, showing interest in, and being involved in the lives of others.

Public Housing

Public housing was established to provide decent and safe rental housing for eligible low-income families, the elderly, and persons with disabilities.[56] Public housing comes in all sizes and types, from scattered single-family houses to high-rise apartments for elderly families. There are approximately 1.2 million households living in public housing units, managed by some 3,300 Housing Authorities.[57] The U.S. Department of Housing and Urban Development (HUD) administers federal aid to local housing agencies (HA) that manage the housing for low-income residents at rents they can afford. HUD furnishes technical and professional assistance in planning, developing, and managing these developments. In the United States, welfare refers more specifically to money paid by the government to persons who need financial assistance.

Theoretical Frameworks

There are four theories that are relevant: Structural Poverty Theory, Geographic Theory, Cumulative/Cyclical Theory, and the Cultural of Poverty Theory. While no one theory will explain all instances of poverty,

---

53 Michael Mintrom, *Public Policy: Why Ethics Matter.* Edited by Jonathan Boston, Andrew Bradstock, and David Eng (ANU E. Press). www.epress.anu.edu.au/ethics (Accessed February 1, 2011).

54 Ibid.

55 Josen and Butler, "Public Ethics and Policy Making," 21.

56 U.S. Department of Housing and Urban Development. www.hud.gov.

57 Ibid.

I use several theories to address poverty. The Making A Difference (MAD) Model is a blended theoretical framework developed from a combination of the Structural, Geographic, and Cumulative/Cyclical theories. The Cultural of Poverty Theory does not address or explain the persistent poverty among African Americans; therefore, the Culture of Poverty Theory has been rejected, and the MAD Framework will guide this research.

Structural Theory

The Structural Theory was selected because it weakens the mainstream's misplaced and misdirected theories that focus solely on individual attributes as the cause of poverty. The Structural Theory doesn't look at the individual as the cause of poverty; it looks at poverty as the result of structural failings at the economic, political, and social levels, which cause people to have limited opportunities and resources to achieve income and well-being.[58] This theory suggests that United States' poverty is largely the result of structural failings which consist of (1) the inability of the U.S. labor market to provide enough decent-paying jobs for all families to avoid poverty or near-poverty; (2) the ineffectiveness of American public policy in reducing levels of poverty via the social safety net; (3) the fact that the majority of Americans will experience poverty during their adult lifetimes, suggesting the systematic nature of U.S. poverty.[59]

The strength of this theory demonstrates that there are not enough well-paying jobs to support all of those who are looking for work. Research has shown that during the past 25 years, the American economy has increasingly produced a larger number of low-paying jobs, jobs that are part-time, and jobs that lack benefits.[60]

Poverty in the United States is a failure of the economic structure that doesn't provide sufficient opportunities to all who are participating in that system, and as a result, millions of families find themselves struggling below or precariously close to the poverty line.[61] This theory demonstrates that there is also a failure at the political and policy level, specifically, within social and economic programs directed toward economically vulnerable populations

58 Greg J. Duncan, *Years of Poverty, Years of Plenty* (Ann Arbor, MI: Institute for Social Research, University of Michigan, 1984).

59 Mark Robert Rank, *ONE NATION, UNDERPRIVILEGED: Why American Poverty Affects Us All* (New York, NY: Oxford University Press, 2004), 53.

60 Karen Seccombe, "Families in Poverty in the 1990s: Trends, Causes, Consequences, and Lessons Learned." *Journal of Marriage and Family* 62 (2000): 1094–1113.

61 Rank, *ONE NATION, UNDERPRIVILEGED*, 53.

that are minimal in their ability to raise families out of poverty. For the past 25 years, Americans have witnessed an overall retrenchment and reduction in the social safety net and these reductions have included a scaling back of the amount of benefits being transferred and a tightening of program eligibility.[62]

According to Robert Rank, failure has nothing to do with the individual; it is the failure at the structural level. Policymakers lose sight of the fact that governments can and do exert a sizeable impact on the extent of poverty within their jurisdictions. As Duncan notes, a complete explanation of why people are poor would require many interrelated theories—theories of family composition, earnings, asset accumulation, transfer programs, and the macroeconomy to name a few. Further complicating the task, a complete poverty theory would need to be based upon the family, while most theories are based upon individuals.[63]

The weaknesses of the Structural Theory are that it doesn't take into account the systematic failure of the school system (contributing toward low achievement, poor graduation rates, and the few who pursue higher education); accountability; and policymakers' negative attitudes toward the poor. This theory fails to explain why numerous policy programs revert to trying to blame or change individual behavior. The Structural Theory was used to guide this scholarship because it explains how systematic barriers prohibit the poor from access and accomplishment to key social institutions, which has nothing to do with the failure of the individual. Once understood by policymakers, they will create more jobs; improve education for the poor; equalize income distributions; remove discrimination bias from housing, banking, education, and employment. Policymakers have redirected society's ills upon easy targets (the least powerful citizens), rather than recognizing the issues or having any concern for the poor. Persistent poverty in the United States will continue to exist through the structural barriers linked to the selection criteria that will directly or indirectly exclude groups of people based on inappropriate standards, such as racial discrimination and institutionalized racism.

Geographic Theory

The Geographic Theory demonstrates that place influences racial differences in poverty. Place is the locus of economic activity and amenities that give

62 Ibid.
63 Ibid.

value to areas.[64] Places are more valuable economically and socially when there is a greater density of economic activity (businesses, jobs), valuable amenities, and public goods (good schools and neighborhoods, parks, low crime, and museums).[65] According to Michael Stoll, having an attachment to places with valuable assets is expected to reduce the risk of poverty. By contrast, living far from these amenities is thought to increase one's risk of being poor. The Geographic Theory of Poverty suggests that social advantages and disadvantages are concentrated in separate areas. Poverty is caused by geographical disparities such as rural poverty, ghetto poverty, urban disinvestment, Southern poverty, Third-World poverty, and other framings of the problem representing a spatial characterization of poverty that exists separate from other theories.[66] This theory explains that people, institutions, and cultures in certain areas lack the resources needed to generate well-being and income, and they lack the power to claim redistribution. The Geographic Theory was selected because it illustrates that there is a considerable amount of social and economic inequality within neighborhoods, which perpetuates racial segregation, isolation, and the concentration of disadvantaged African Americans.[67] It explains that racial groups, in particular whites and blacks, are residentially segregated. According to Michael Stoll, the persistence of poverty in central cities reinforces the notion that place might matter in influencing such poverty.

According to Massey and Denton, many racially segregated neighborhoods are disadvantaged and suffer disproportionately from problems such as high concentrations of poverty, joblessness, hopelessness, and the political indifference of elites. Research shows that segregated neighborhoods impose enormous costs on minority residents, such as the unavailability of good schools, worse health outcomes, negative role models, a lack of economic opportunities, and social isolation.[68] The weakness of this theory is that more research is needed to address the issue of race, place, and poverty.

According to Wendy Shaw, space is not a backdrop for capitalism; it is restructured by it and contributes to the system's survival. The geography

64 Michael A. Stoll, "Race, Place, and Property Revisited." In *The Colors of Poverty: Why Racial and Ethnic Disparities Persist.* Edited by Ann Chih Lin and David R. Harris (New York, NY: Russell Sage Foundation, 2008), 202.

65 Ibid., 203.

66 R. Asen, *Visions of Poverty: Welfare Policy and Political Imagination* (East Lansing, MI: Michigan State University Press, 2002), 12.

67 Stoll, "Race, Place, and Property Revisited."

68 Massey and Denton, *American Apartheid.*

of poverty is a spatial expression of the capitalist system.[69] Goldsmith and Blakely argue that the joint processes of the movement of households and jobs away from poor areas in central cities and rural regions created a "separation of work, residence, economic, social and political life." These processes are multiplied by racism and political indifference of the localities in which they flourish.[70] According to W. J. Wilson's book *The Truly Disadvantaged*, the people from ghetto areas with the highest levels of education, the greatest skills, the widest worldview, and with the most extensive opportunities were the ones who migrated out of central city locations to other places.

Cumulative and Cyclical Theory

The Cumulative and Cyclical Theory of Poverty was selected because it builds on the components of each of the aforementioned theories; it links economic factors at the individual level with the structural factors that operate at the geographical level. The Cyclical Theory of Poverty demonstrates how multiple problems accumulate, by looking at the individual and their community as caught in a spiral of opportunity and problems, and once problems dominate, they close other opportunities and create a cumulative set of problems that make any effective response nearly impossible.[71] This theory has its origins in economics in the work of Gunnar Myrdal, who developed a theory of interlocking, circular, interdependence within a process of cumulative causation that helps to explain economic underdevelopment and development. According to Myrdal, personal and community well-being are closely related and the interdependence of factors creating poverty accelerates once a cycle of decline has started. This theory was selected to help guide this study because it explains the spirals of poverty; the problems for individuals (such as earnings, housing, health, education, and self-confidence) are interdependent and strongly linked to community deficiencies (such as loss of business, jobs, inadequate schools, and the inability to provide social services).[72]

The limitation of the Cyclical Theory of Poverty is its complexity, but the problem is that the linkages and interdependence are hard to break because each is reinforced by other parts of the spiraling system. Community-level

---

69 W. Shaw, *The Geography of United States Poverty* (New York, NY: Garland Publishing, 1996).

70 Ibid.

71 Ted K. Bradshaw, "Complex Community Development Projects: Collaboration, Comprehensive Programs and Community Coalitions in Complex Society." *Community Development Journal* 35, no. 2 (2001): 133–145.

72 Ibid., 136.

crisis leads to individual crisis and vice versa, and each accumulates, causing spirals of poverty.

Culture of Poverty Theory

The Culture of Poverty Theory is a social theory explaining the cycle of poverty. It suggests that poverty is caused by a subculture that adopts values that are non-productive and contrary to the norms of success.[73] Oscar Lewis was the first to popularize the concept of the "culture of poverty." He described it as a way of life; a combination of certain traits passed on through generations; an adaptation to poverty and "being at the bottom" in an industrialized, capitalist society perpetuating itself once started. The Culture of Poverty is defined as an adaptation and a reaction of the poor to their marginal position in a class-stratified, highly individualistic, capitalist society.[74] The essence of the Culture of Poverty theory holds that poor people share deviant cultural characteristics and have lifestyles that differ from the rest of society, which perpetuates their life of poverty. The Culture of Poverty weaknesses tend to present negative connotations and characteristics about the poor that are highly stereotypical, all sharing the belief that defects are passed from one generation to the next, and once under these circumstances, it is extremely difficult for people, once trapped by the Culture of Poverty, to escape poverty.

According to the Moynihan Report (1965), the Culture of Poverty is a functionalist approach to poverty. It assumes a "right" or "correct" culture and a deviant culture. The poor are poor and are likely to remain poor because their culture deviates from the norm. The Moynihan Report is a study that borrows aspects of the Culture of Poverty to explain African American poverty in the United States. Its goal was to explain the continued poverty during the 1960s. The Moynihan Study pointed out that much of the poverty associated with the Black community was due to a history of slavery and economic oppression (unemployment). It also called attention to the necessity of altering one's lifestyle as a means to cope with poverty. The weakness of the report is that it places the blame for poverty on the victim, which removes it from society as a duty of the government and once poverty is viewed as the fault of the poor and not the government, their culture, not social injustice, causes and perpetuates poverty. The implied assumption is that until the poor

73 Ted K. Bradshaw, "Theories of Poverty and Anti-Poverty Programs in Community Development." Rural Poverty Research Center, August 2005. www.rprconline.org.

74 Oscar Lewis, *La Vida: A Puerto Rican Family in the Culture of Poverty* (New York, NY: Random House, 1966).

change their "culture," no amount of government intervention will solve the problem of poverty.

The results of the Moynihan Report and the Culture of Poverty Theory paved the way for policymakers to perform their social duties, which have guided policies in a certain direction. The cultural roots of poverty have played an important role in shaping policy and how lawmakers choose to address poverty issues.[75] The 1960s were a decade in which poverty in the United States was blamed on the victim and the culture of poverty flourished. The underlying argument of conservatives implied that the welfare system perpetuated poverty by permitting a cycle of "welfare dependency," where poor families developed and passed on to others, the skills needed to work the system rather than to gain paying employment.[76] Some scholars believed that a Culture of Poverty exists while others denied it. According to Oscar Lewis, there were always contradictions when evaluating the poor, which stemmed from the power struggle of competing groups and their failure to distinguish between poverty and a culture of poverty, which is an adaptation to certain common problems or traits among families with the lowest income levels and the least education.[77] According to Patricia Cohen, Moynihan's analysis never lost its appeal to conservative thinkers, whose arguments ultimately succeeded when, in 1996, President Bill Clinton signed a bill into law "ending welfare as we know it." However, after decades of silence, these scholars are speaking openly about the culture of poverty, conceding that culture and persistent poverty are enmeshed.[78]

Scholars suggest that a Culture of Poverty exists among African Americans because of their lack of a work ethic, inappropriate family values, ethic of dependency, and/or their personal inadequacies, suggesting that it passes from one generation to the next without looking into some of the root causes such as an industrial capitalist society along with its inherent inequalities in wage labor and production for a profit; a high rate of unemployment; underemployment for unskilled labor; low wages, and a failure to provide social, political, economic organization for the low-income population. Research indicates that the poor do not differ from the better-off part of society in their values, and that there are various sources of possible inequalities, not only from the cash income from wages but from assets, private income, and

75 Patricia Cohen, "Culture of Poverty Makes a Comeback." *The New York Times*, October 17, 2010. www.nytimes.com.

76 Asen, *Visions of Poverty*.

77 Oscar Lewis, *Anthropology Essays* (New York, NY: Random House, 1970).

78 Cohen, "Culture of Poverty Makes a Comeback."

employment benefits. Culture of Poverty proponents argue that the poor adapt to a lifestyle that allows them to deal with poverty. They tend to assume that once these lifestyles have been adopted, they become institutionalized with poor culture, making it very difficult for the poor to escape the culture of poverty. One might ask that if it is so easy to adapt to poverty lifestyles, that it might be just as easy to adapt to a middle-class lifestyle once that lifestyle is provided.

Methodology

The primary methodology utilized in this scholarship is qualitative. Qualitative studies are described as being a type of research that produces findings not arrived at by means of statistical procedures or other means of quantification.[79] Qualitative research can be used to better understand phenomenon about what little is known.[80] A case study approach has been chosen to elicit more in-depth information on what causes persistent poverty among African Americans in the United States. The case study approach was utilized to determine if government programs and federal policies have helped or hindered African Americans in moving in and out of poverty. It is an appropriate strategy used to answer questions that ask how and why but does not require control over the events.[81] A case study can be defined as an empirical inquiry that investigates a contemporary phenomenon within its real-life context, when the boundaries between phenomenon and context are not clearly evident.[82] The case study used in this scholarship is based upon an interpretive framework. An interpretive framework is one in which understanding the meaning of a process or experience constitutes the knowledge to be gained from an inductive mode of inquiry rather than a deductive (hypothesis or theory testing) mode.[83]

A single-case study approach was used to address the research questions, to determine whether a theory's propositions are correct or whether some alternative set of explanations might be more relevant. Using a single case-study

79 A. Strauss and J. Corbin, *Basics of Qualitative Research: Grounded Theory Procedures and Techniques* (Newbury Park, CA: Sage Publications, Inc., 1990), 17.

80 Ibid., 18.

81 C. Robson, *Real World Research: A Resource for Social Scientist and Practicioner-Researchers* (London: Blackwell, 1993), 57.

82 Robert Yin, *A Case Study Research: Design and Methods. Applied Social Research Methods* (Thousand Oaks, CA: Sage Publications, Inc., 2009), 13.

83 S. B. Merriam, *Qualitative Research and Case Study Application in Education* (San Francisco, CA: Jossey-Bass Publisher, 1988), 32.

can represent a significant contribution to knowledge, theory building, and can help with future investigations in an entire field. The targeted population for this research was African American citizens in the United States that have remained in persistent poverty. A policy analysis was used as a criterion to measure policy performance, which highlighted the effectiveness and/or ineffectiveness of each policy, to determine if it helped or hindered African Americans in the United States. The use of a policy analysis identified models and alternative solutions. Examining Lyndon B. Johnson's War on Poverty programs and policies as a case study has determined that policies made a difference in creating or lessening/eliminating poverty among African Americans. Data triangulation was utilized to collect multiple sources of evidence that address a broader range of historical and behavioral issues, as well as data and facts that addressed each question. This technique has advanced the research through the use of documentation, archival records, interviews, direct observations, participant observation, and surveys.

The case-study approach is one of several ways of doing social science research. Each strategy has peculiar advantages and disadvantages. The strengths of a case study allows the investigator to research the present social phenomenon, without relying on the past; it allows direct observation of the events being studied and interviews of individuals involved in the events or of some significance to the case study; a major strength of case-study data collection is the opportunity to use many different sources of evidence that include documents, artifacts, interviews, observations; and it explains the presumed causal links in real-life interventions that may be too complex for surveys or experimental strategies.

The weaknesses of a case study may promote an informal manipulation of the data from the researcher that may allow the investigator to create or dismiss data because of individual bias; the researcher has no control over the events; case study investigators may lack the skill for investigating; and may hold biased views that influence the direction of the findings/conclusions.

Documentary information is likely to be relevant to every case-study topic.[84] Documentation may be useful, stable, broad, and exact in providing unobtrusive evidence that supports other data within the case study.[85] The documents for this case study include agendas, announcements, reports, proposals, progress reports, and formal studies or evaluations from Lyndon B. Johnson's unconditional War on Poverty and Great Society Legislation, with a comparison to the present social policies used today in the United States

84 Yin, *A Case Study Research*, 80.

85 Ibid.

created to eliminate or lessen poverty. Documentation has various advantages such as a broad coverage of many events, a long span of time, and within many settings; it provides exact names, references, and details of an event. However, disadvantages of documentation aren't obsolete, retrievable information may be difficult to find, access may be deliberately blocked, and there may be biased selectivity of information. For many case studies, archival records often in a computerized form may also be relevant. Archival sources can produce qualitative and quantitative information. Archival records may include service records, such as showing the number of clients served over a given period of time; organizational records, such as organizational charts and budgets over a period of time; survey data, such as census records or data previously collected about a "site"; and maps and charts of the geographical characteristics of a place.[86]

The U.S. Census data was used in this case study to define who is poor in the United States by race, gender, and demographics since the passing of the Great Society Legislation. Service records, organizational records, and maps and charts used during the 1960s have provided relevant information on social policies, the budgets, and clients served over a specific period of time.

Existing Literature

There is a wealth of literature on the causes of poverty. The Institute for Research on Poverty at the University of Wisconsin, established in 1966, has published more than 40 books and 800 papers on the topic. Robert Haveman concludes that in terms of both inputs (research expenditures) and outputs (journal articles), poverty-related research has grown substantially since the mid-1960s. Important literature includes work done by Ann Chih Lin and David R. Harris, *The Colors of Poverty: Why Racial and Ethnic Disparities Persist*; Sheldon H. Danziger and Robert Haveman, *Understanding Poverty*; William Julius Wilson, *The Truly Disadvantaged: The Inner City, the Underclass, and Public Policy*; Charles Murray, *Losing Ground: American Social Policy, 1950–1980*; Maria Cancian and Sheldon Danziger, *Changing Poverty, Changing Policies*; Michael A. Stoll, "Race, Place, and Poverty," and Isabel V. Sawhill, "Poverty In The U.S. Why Is It So Persistent?". These works are important because each of these authors has made an enormous contribution to the study of poverty and policy in the United States. Each of these works has shown the most important factors that have influenced disadvantage and persistent poverty among African Americans such as the federal government, its power and policies,

86 Ibid., 83.

which were created to lessen or eliminate poverty, but have actually worsened poverty.

According to Ann Chih Lin and David R. Harris, American social policy after the 1960s has continued to disadvantage African Americans, and in some cases Latinos, relative to white Americans. In Joe Soss and Sandy Schram's article titled, "Coloring the Terms of Membership," they viewed place as the potential for policy to perpetuate racial disparities in its broader historical and political context. In Scott Allard's article titled, "Place, Race, and Access to the Safety Net," he explores welfare as the pragmatic case of poverty policy. Some of the literature states that the problem of poverty in the United States is also a problem of color. It becomes important to consider the significance of discrimination in the context of persistent poverty among members of racial or ethnic minority groups. Devah Pager suggests that discrimination remains an important source of disadvantage for many minority groups, contributing to limited opportunities in employment, housing, consumer markets, health care, and many other domains.

The term "culture" figures prominently in the literature on poverty, race, and ethnicity without much theoretical or empirical sophistication.[87] In the literature, culture is conceived rather vaguely as a group's norms and values, as its attitudes toward work and family, or as its observed patterns of behavior. Culture has been discussed by many poverty experts without depth or precision of their analyses of matters such as demographic trends, selection bias, or the impact of public policies on work and family structure.[88] This lack of sophistication is reflected in many practices, such as the use of culture and race interchangeably, the belief that all members of a racial group share a unified set of beliefs or patterns of behavior, or the use of culture as a residual category to explain unaccounted for variance statistical model, or the use of culture exclusively as an intermediary mechanism.[89] By contrast, other scholars reject cultural explanations altogether, arguing that a culture cannot be studied scientifically or that cultural explanations inevitably blame the victims for their problems.[90] Poverty scholarship tends to reveal a rather thin understanding of culture. This literature has not united into a coherent

87 Michele Lamont and Mario Luis Small, "How Culture Matters: Enriching Our Understanding of Poverty." In *The Colors of Poverty: Why Racial and Ethnic Disparities Persist.* Edited by Ann Chih and David R. Harris (New York, NY: The Russell Sage Foundation, 2008), 76.

88 Ibid.

89 William Julius Wilson, *The Truly Disadvantaged: The Inner City, the Underclass, and Public Policy* (Chicago, IL: The University of Chicago Press, 1987).

90 Lamont and Small, "How Culture Matters," 77.

perspective on culture, but all of these approaches will allow social scientists to move beyond the assumption that racial groups have inherent cultural traits, such as an Asian work ethic.[91]

The literature shows that poverty rates are higher among minorities for a variety of reasons which include limited access to educational opportunities and inherited wealth, racial discrimination in housing and labor markets, and a disconnect from networks that generate economic rewards. These are major factors that account for some of the higher poverty rates of minority groups. The research is consistent with the idea that place influences poverty (or opportunity) given that in the United States, minority groups are more likely to live in rural and central areas.[92] According to Michael Stoll and the literature, the persistence of poverty in the central city reinforces the notion that place plays a role in influencing poverty. Public policy has also contributed to the factors that influence persistent poverty among African Americans and their communities.

In Maria Cancian and Sheldon Danziger's book titled, *Changing Poverty and Changing Policies*, they suggest that poverty persists not because the War on Poverty planners were fundamentally mistaken, but because the changing economy increased economic hardships for many workers and the existing antipoverty policies did not respond sufficiently to offset market-generated increases in poverty. Policies also failed to respond adequately to the largely unanticipated changes in family organization. New analyses in the literature suggest that poverty should not remain high and that certain antipoverty policies, if undertaken, can effectively reduce poverty far below its current levels.[93]

91 Ibid.

92 Stoll, "Race Place and Poverty Revisited."

93 Maria Cancian and Sheldon Danziger, *Changing Poverty and Changing Policies* (New York, NY: Russell Sage Foundation, 2009).

Chapter 2

WHAT ARE THE SCHOLARS SAYING ABOUT POVERTY?

In the United States, the impact of public policies has hindered African Americans, causing them to remain deprived and disadvantaged. Prejudice, discrimination, and inequality have contributed significantly to the persistence of poverty among African Americans. The literature and past research illustrate that not all Americans were treated equally, particularly in the labor, housing, and education markets, and it is not coincidental that minorities comprise a disproportionate number of the poverty population.[1] The U.S. Census Bureau reports that white Americans have the lowest poverty rates (8.6 percent), while African Americans have the highest poverty rates (17.1 percent).[2] This chapter provides a review of the relevant literature on the causes and extent of persistent poverty among African Americans in the United States.

Political Approaches/Explanations to Understanding Poverty

Richard Roper's book, *Persistent Poverty: The American Dream Turned Nightmare*, provides an understanding of what constitutes poverty, what it means to be poor, and how extensive poverty actually is in the United States. Richard Roper provides a thorough investigation of the factors contributing to poverty; which include the lack of affordable housing, low-paying jobs, deindustrialization, and irregular employment for African Americans. He provides insight into the fact that many impoverished people draw regular paychecks and are gainfully employed, but neither their compensation nor their political or economic circumstances can pull them above the poverty line, creating

1 Richard H. Ropers, *Persistent Poverty: The American Dream Turned Nightmare* (New York, NY: Insight Books, Plenum Press, 1991), 182.
2 U.S. States Census Bureau. http://www.census.gov.

victims of poverty.[3] According to Roper, social welfare programs that were designed to serve the poor have been significantly reduced, destroying the safety net for the poorest Americans.[4]

In an array of previous studies, researchers have argued that there are two political approaches to understanding the causes of poverty, each of which provides distinct types of information. Richard Roper focused on two schools of thought that formed the foundation for most political responses and non-responses to the problem of poverty. The first approach is blaming the victim/individual and the second approach is blaming the system. Roper views poverty as an institutional cause, not as an individual's failure. In the first approach, blaming the victim, he argued that there are two issues that generate controversy: its scientific validity and its ideological role.[5] William Ryan, in Blaming the Victim, was one of the first to suggest that a category of theories exists to account for various social problems, which focus on the characteristics, attributes, and behaviors of those individuals who suffer from specific social problems. William Ryan refers to blaming the victim approach as a "process of evasion." He argues that the process of evasion is a distraction from the structural causes of poverty, leaving primary injustice untouched.[6]

Many explanations for the existence of poverty have been offered in the literature. William W. Goldsmith and Edward J. Blakely reduce the theories and explanations of poverty into three categories: (1) poverty as a pathology, (2) poverty as an incident or accident, and (3) poverty as a structure.[7] These explanations of poverty are reflected in the writings of many social welfare researchers, such as Michael Sherraden, Bradley Schiller, and Chaim I. Waxman, who all place the elaborate theories and various themes of poverty into two groups: theories that focus on individual behaviors and theories that focus on social structures.[8,9,10] Another set of researchers suggests that there are two basic subsets of blaming the victim approach, the liberal view and the conservative view. One liberal variant is reflected in the work of sociologist

---

3 Wayne K. Hinton, Foreword. Ropers, Richard H. *Persistent Poverty: The American Dream Turned Nightmare* (New York, NY: Insight Books, Plenum Press, 1991).

4 Ibid., 2.

5 Ibid., 115.

6 Ibid.

7 William W. Goldsmith and Edward J. Blakely, *Separate Societies: Poverty and Inequality in U.S. Cities* (Philadelphia, PA: Temple University Press, 1992).

8 Michael Sherraden, *Assets and the Poor* (Armonk, NY: M.E. Sharpe Press, 1991), 35.

9 Bradley Schiller, *The Economics of Poverty and Discrimination* (Upper Saddle River, NJ: Pearson Prentice-Halls, Inc., 2004).

10 Chaim Waxman, *Stigma of Poverty: A Critique of Poverty Theories and Policies* (Elmsford, NY: Pegamon Press, 1983).

Oscar Lewis. In Oscar Lewis's book *La Vida: A Puerto Rican Family in the Culture of Poverty*, he argued that the poor are poor because they do not have middle-class norms and values; and they have not been allowed to develop the proper values and behaviors for achieving middle-class status in the United States. In Edward C. Banfield's book *The Unheavenly City Revisited*, he provides a conservative perspective on the explanation of poverty. Banfield argues that the innate "ethos" of some groups prevents them from acquiring the proper work habits, moral dispositions, attitudes, and cultural norms necessary for social mobility, regardless of the government's attempts to achieve this. According to Banfield, the government should not waste resources trying to change the innate cultural weaknesses of some people, but should seek to constrain their physical mobility and their ability to damage the chances of others in the black community. According to Manuel Carballo and Mary Jo Bane, conservatives from the Thomas Hobbes era to the present day have felt that the causes and cures of individual poverty are essentially not political or economic, but moral. Conservatives suggest that anyone who is willing to work hard can make it and those who haven't made it must be unwilling to work and are lazy. Both argue that this theme has influenced every conservative solution to poverty in the United States.[11]

A significant piece of literature relates to blaming the victim theories and has several themes in common. All are reductionist, accounting for the complex social conditions of poverty, homelessness, inequality, and stratification in terms of genetic, biological, attitudinal, or personality defects and pathology. All are overly simplistic, limited in their scientific validity, and lend themselves to supporting conservative views. Conservatives define poverty as the product of individual failings and a consequence of one's own personal inadequacies and they will not blame the "system" for what they see as the moral failures of individuals.[12] C. Emory Burton concludes that conservative interpretations of poverty may be rejected outright because there is little or no empirical support for such claims.[13] He argues that whatever deviant cultural values some of the poor may hold are a result rather than a cause of their condition. According to Oscar Lewis, the culture of poverty "is an indictment not of the poor, but of the social system that produces this way of life."

11 Manuel Carballo and Mary Jo Bane, *The State and the Poor in the 1980s* (Westport, CT: Auburn Publishing, 1984).

12 Henry J. Hyde, "Morals, Markets and Freedoms." *National Review* 42, no. 21 (November 1990): 52–54.

13 Emory C. Burton, *The Poverty Debate: Politics and the Poor in America* (Westport, CT: Praeger Publishers, 1992), 37.

Blaming the Victim Approach: Conservative Views

Christopher Jencks and Paul Patterson use the term "undeserving poor" and indicate that their poverty is somehow attributed to their behavior.[14] According to Henry Hazlitt, poverty is ultimately individual, and each individual or family must solve its own problems of poverty. In his book titled, *Wealth and Poverty*, George Gilder implies that the poor are different, many are black, their IQs are genetically lower, and they are markedly prone to violence, crime, and slovenly living. Charles Murray, in his book *Losing Ground*, argued that well-intentioned governmental policies and programs have "trapped" the poor into a cycle of persistent poverty and welfare dependency, which has resulted in higher poverty rates among the poor. According to Murray, the poor are those who avoid work, are amoral, and should be held responsible for their actions. Lawrence Mead refers to an element of the poor as street hustlers, welfare families, drug addicts, and former mental patients who will not take jobs.[15]

The 1965 Moynihan Report on the Negro Family linked the social problems among blacks such as joblessness, illegitimacy, and juvenile delinquency, to the increasing rates of female-headed households in black families. Critics accused Moynihan of stigmatizing blacks, "blaming the victim," and ignoring the consequences of societal racism. Chaim Waxman in *The Stigma of Poverty* argued that the poor were less than successful, not because of their culture, but because of their stigmatization and isolation. He acknowledges that a "deviant subculture" exists among the poor, but he believes it to be situational.[16] According to William J. Wilson, cultural traits exist, but it is a response to the social structural constraints and opportunities.[17] Wilson also claimed that this controversy has led liberal scholars to avoid discussing behavioral issues that might be construed as unflattering to minorities, and as a result, by the 1980s conservatives dominated the intellectual discussions about poverty, blaming the individual and their behavioral problems as the origin of poverty. William J. Wilson disputes blaming the victim ideas and explanations of poverty put forth by neoconservatives such as Charles Murray, George Gilder, Edward Banfield, and others, arguing that the key

14 Christopher Jencks and Paul Patterson, *The Urban Underclass* (Washington, DC: The Brookings Institute, 1991).

15 Lawrence Mead, *Beyond Entitlement: The Social Obligations of Citizenship* (New York, NY: The Free Press, 1986).

16 Waxman, *Stigma of Poverty*, 126.

17 William Julius Wilson, *The Truly Disadvantaged: The Inner City, the Underclass, and the Public Policy* (Chicago, IL: Chicago University Press, 1987), 61.

theoretical concept is not the individual or a culture of poverty, but social isolation and joblessness. He argues that the poor will not conform to the norms of the middle class because they have become detached from specific sectors of society and are increasingly isolated from role models who reflect acceptable social behavior. Charles A. Valentine argues that E. Franklin Frazier's sociological work laid much of the foundation for the culture of poverty perspective and argues that those who propose cultural differences as explanations for poverty have not analytically proved their cases.[18]

Blaming the System Approach: Views from the Left

Throughout the literature, poverty is viewed as persistent because it is considered an integral component of the economic and social institutions in the United States. The bureaucratic systems in operation that are supposed to help lessen or eliminate poverty have aggravated the conditions and problems of the poor.[19] Many empirical studies have demonstrated that the poor have problems with health, alcoholism, drug abuse, emotional instability, subcultural attitudes, and behaviors that deviate from "middle-class" norms. Blaming the System approach views all of those problems as the effect, not as the cause, of poverty.[20] Blaming the System approach removes the blame from the individual and places it on the political and economic systems in the United States.

In *Living Poorly in America*, Leonard Beeghley identified being poor as part of a vicious cycle that traps people and prevents their escape from poverty.[21] According to Beeghley, there are significant elements of that vicious cycle such as pauperism and political disenfranchisement. He argued that the government should stimulate impoverished households to remove people from poverty instead of creating antipoverty policies that have been designed to keep them poor.[22] Beeghley indicated in his work that destitute persons are politically disfranchised because they do not have the resources necessary to participate in the legitimate political arena and major political parties make no effort to mobilize impoverished persons. He argues that "welfare" policy benefits the middle class and penalizes the poor for working; public assistance does not promote family stability; street crime is not controlled; and the

18 Ropers, *Persistent Poverty*, 200.
19 Ibid.
20 Ibid.
21 Leonard Beeghley, *Living Poorly In America* (New York, NY: Praeger Publishers, 1983), 134.
22 Ibid.

healthcare delivery system does not meet the needs of the poor.[23] Beeghley argues that patterns of racial discrimination are not accidental and the structural mechanism of society simply reflects the ability of a class system dominated by white males, which reproduces itself over time. And because of this, regardless of the level of achievement or the degree of labor force participation, blacks are much more likely to live below the poverty level than whites.[24]

William Julius Wilson in *The Truly Disadvantaged* argued that the plight of poor blacks results more often from their social-class membership than from their race. According to Wilson, middle-class blacks have benefited from the civil rights movement, changes in the policies and laws regarding discrimination, while working-class blacks have remained trapped in a lower-class system that has been produced by large economic and social trends, in which the poor have no immediate control. He argued that the working-class and lower-class blacks have experienced higher rates of unemployment and underemployment due to the changes in the economy and the exit of industries out of the central cities. Herbert J. Gans's argument in "The Uses of Poverty: The Poor Pay All" moves the argument in a different direction, as he argued that poverty persists because it has certain positive functions for particular segments in American society that do not benefit the nation as a whole. He states that poverty

> makes possible the existence or expansion of respectable professions and occupations, for example, penology, criminology, social work and public health. [...] The poor have provided jobs for professional and paraprofessional "poverty warriors," and for journalist and social scientist [...] who have supplied information demanded by the revival of public interest in poverty.

In Gans's opinion, the functions of poverty and inequality serve a purpose for the middle and upper classes. It ensures that society's dirty work gets done; that the poor will subsidize the middle and upper classes by working for low wages and paying a disproportionate amount of taxes; that poverty creates many professional jobs in social work, counseling, law enforcement; and that the poor buy goods and services that otherwise would be rejected in society: for example, day-old bread, and receiving services from old, retired, or incompetent professionals. Furthermore, with the poor being politically powerless, they are forced to absorb the cost of change and growth in American society. Gans strongly implies that these "functions" of poverty motivate

23 Ibid., 135.
24 Ibid., 156.

those members of society who benefit from them to find ways of ensuring that poverty persists.[25]

In *The Sociological Imagination*, C. Wright Mills wrote:

> When, in a city of 100,000, only one man is unemployed, that is his personal trouble, and for its relief we properly look to the character of the man, his skills, and his immediate opportunities. But when in a nation of 50 million employees, 15 million men are unemployed, that is an issue, and we may not hope to find its solution within the range of opportunities open to any one individual. The very structure of opportunities has collapsed. Both the correct statement of the problems and the range of possible solutions require us to consider the economic and political institutions of the society, and not merely the personal situation and character of a scatter of individuals.

Many writers have argued vigorously for and against attacks on the poor, either blaming the victim or blaming the system. The U.S. Census Bureau reports that millions of Americans are living below the poverty line, and millions more are hovering just above it. However, it would seem that blaming the victim theories constitute at best incomplete, and at worst simply false, misleading explanations for these conditions. Although the poor seem to threaten the smug security and illusions of the middle and upper classes, blaming the system explanations offer greater insight into the reality of American society.[26]

An interesting finding in the literature implies that being born into a black family rather than into a white family dramatically reduces a child's adult economic prospects. According to Cochran, a vast majority of black children will be poor, will live in a family that receives welfare, and will live in a single-parent home at some point during their childhood. A large minority of black children will live in these situations for a period of time during their childhood, which will lead to significantly lower adult economic attainment.[27] Similarly, Michael Harrington observed more than 20 years ago,

> The real explanation of why the poor are where they are is that they made the mistake of being born to the wrong parents, in the wrong section of the country, in the wrong industry, or to the wrong racial or ethnic group. Once that mistake has been made, they could have been

25 Herbert J. Gans, "The Uses of Poverty: The Poor Pay All." *Social Policy* (July/August 1971): 78–81.

26 Ropers, *Persistent Poverty*, 171.

27 M. Corcoran, "Rags to Rags: Poverty and Mobility in the United States." *Annual Review of Sociology* 21 (1995): 245.

paragons of will and morality, but most of them would never even have a chance to get out of the other America.[28]

Persistent Poverty and Policy

James Jennings and Louis Kushnick's book of anthologies titled *A New Introduction to Poverty: The Role of Race, Power, and Politics*, reveals some of the essential literature explaining the nature and causes of persistent poverty among specific groups in the United States. They illustrate why persistent poverty cannot be understood completely or reduced significantly without examining the question of who has political influence in the United States. Both argue that the unchanging distribution of wealth and power is the greatest determinant of persistent poverty among particular sectors in society that generally keep high proportions of women and people of color in economically vulnerable and impoverished positions.[29] They argue that the causes of poverty are exacerbated by national policies that allow corporate leaders to pursue profits without consideration of the social costs incurred by their strategies.

According to Jennings and Kushnick, in the United States, there are various tools and mechanisms used to silence the class tensions that arise from the subsidization of the rich by the working and middle-class sectors of the population. The tools used for this purpose include segregation and discrimination; the belief and practices associated with the presumption of white cultural superiority; political and racial scapegoating; public presentation/dialogue, and welfare reform today.[30] Jennings and Kushnick argue that there are at least three mechanisms to the causes of poverty. First is the ideological belief, in which diligent individuals can make it economically and achieve the good life if they work hard and put God and country above everything else; second is the supply-side proposition, which maintains that economic development and progress will result from allowing the wealthy interest to accumulate more wealth by implementing policies that will result in lower taxes and less regulation of income ensuring that the wealthy will have more resources to save and invest; and race is the third, which class tensions and popular dissatisfaction along with economic policies have been managed and manipulated by the wealthy and powerful interests used to divide the poor

---

28 Michael Harrington, *The Other America* (Baltimore, MD: Penguin Books, 1971).

29 Louis Kushnick and James Jennings (eds.), *A New Introduction to Poverty: The Role of Race, Power, and Politics* (New York, NY and London: University Press, 1999). (Introduction)

30 Ibid., 5.

black working-class people from the poor working-class people who are not black.

Poverty and Race

James Jennings and Louis Kushnick argued that the racialization of poverty is strengthened and facilitated by private and public policies that continue to result in residential and educational segregation. They illustrate that there are significant differences among black, white, Latino, Asian, and Native American poverty in the United States. According to Jennings and Kushnick, black poverty tends to be more highly concentrated; black people are impoverished for longer periods of time than whites; black poor people tend to be poorer than white poor people; and black and Latino children remain the most impoverished throughout the United States. Both agreed that the root causes of persistent poverty are linked directly to the political and economic structures in society.

Many explanations for the existence of poverty have been offered in the literature. In *The Economics of Poverty and Discrimination*, Bradley R. Schiller refers to poverty as the "restricted opportunity" argument. He proposes that the poor are poor because they do not have adequate access to good schools, jobs, or income, and because they are discriminated against on the basis of color, sex, income, or class, and they are not afforded a fair share of government protection, subsidy, or services.

The historian, Jay R. Mandel, in *The Roots of Black Poverty*, provides a historic explanation for black poverty, which is a variation of the restricted-opportunity thesis proposed by Schiller. Mandel correctly points out that black poverty certainly existed during slavery and has persisted continually since Emancipation. He argues that family structure and group attitudes or attributes may have changed over generations, but poverty has consistently been more widespread and persistent among black Americans than it has been among white Americans. Mandel explains in his work that continuing black poverty is a reflection and continuation of the effects of the plantation economy in the South that persisted for decades after the Civil War.[31] This echoes the analysis by W. E. B. Du Bois in his classic work, *Black Reconstruction in America 1860–1880* in which Du Bois states that, "it was the policy of the state to keep the Negro laborer poor, to confine him as far as possible to menial occupation, to make him a surplus labor reservoir and to force him

31 Jay R. Mandel, *The Roots of Black Poverty: The Southern Plantation Economy After the Civil War* (Durham, NC: Duke University Press, 1978).

into peonage and unpaid toil."[32,33] Mandel argues that the effects of the plantation economy have prevented millions of blacks from developing the political tools and economic positions they needed to obtain control of parts of the emerging industrialized order.

Racism and discrimination cannot be discounted or dismissed as explanations for persistent poverty in African American communities. In a report published by political scientist Anthony Downs, titled *Who Are the Urban Poor?*, he identified several ways in which institutions discriminated against poor people, especially blacks in particular. They include providing assistance in ways that emphasized dependency; imposing higher costs for goods and services; omitting impoverished people from social insurance schemes; denying services (mortgage loans, credit, municipal services); and maintaining public schools of lower quality. Manuel Carballo states that the failure to take account of racism and discrimination is a major weakness in how conservatives approach the problem of poverty:

> The central mission element, by omission or commission, in the conservative view of poverty, drawn as it is from the intellectual roots of a then racially homogenous Great Britain, is its failure to grasp the basic relationship in multi-racial America between racism and poverty. While most of the poor are white, disproportionate numbers of the poor are black, Hispanic and Native American. [...] Racism is by no means the sole or perhaps even the primary cause of poverty among minorities. [...] But racism does have a lot to do with the concentration of minorities in municipalities whose tax base cannot carry quality public education; in neighborhoods that make minorities the disproportionate victims of crime; in jobs that are part-time, low-wage, and without the benefits of health insurance, pensions, or even social security.[34]

In *Where Do We Go from Here: Chaos or Community?* Martin Luther King Jr., defined the nature of persistent poverty fundamentally as a reflection of the political power and moral will of the wealthy and better-off sectors in society. He argued that only political power on the part of the poor could solve the problem of poverty in the United States. According to Martin Luther King Jr., United States capitalism or the excesses of capitalism, rather than

---

32 W. E. B. DuBois, *Black Reconstruction in America, 1860–1880* (New York, NY: Atheneum Press, 1985), 696. Originally Published in 1935.

33 Kushnick and Jennings (eds), *A New Introduction to Poverty.*

34 Carballo and Bane, *The State and the Poor in the 1980s.*

individual or group deficiencies, produces and is responsible for poverty in the United States.

Housing and Policy

The literature confirms that the federal government and individual housing authorities have played an active and deliberate role in concentrating poverty in racially segregated neighborhoods that are located far from amenities, shopping, or services. According to the United States 2000 Periodic Report, the federal government was responsible for promoting racial discrimination in housing for many years.[35] In 1934, the federal government used the Federal Housing Administration's (FHA) mortgage insurance programs to transform the housing market from one that was effectively inaccessible to people outside the upper-middle classes, to a broad-based one, for whites only.[36] The FHA, in combination with the New Deal-era selective credit programs, had a huge impact on the housing market, which functioned to insure private lenders against loss, standardized appraisal practices, and popularized the use of long-term amortized mortgages. The aforementioned policies and practices that were used to create and perpetuate patterns of residential segregation and persistent poverty among African Americans are still in existence today.[37] According to Michael Katz, the federal government manipulated market incentives in ways that lured middle-class whites into the suburbs and trapped blacks in the inner cities, creating their stagnation and persistent poverty. According to Michael Stoll, the persistence of poverty in the central city reinforces the notion that place does indeed play a role in influencing poverty.

In Rod Solomon's article, "Public Housing Reform and Voucher Success: Progress and Challenges," he argued that most public housing built from the 1950s to the 1970s was comprised of large, densely populated "projects," often consisting of high-rise buildings located in poor, racially segregated communities. John M. Goering, in *Housing Desegregation And Federal Policy*, argued that Housing and Urban Development (HUD) is and has admitted to being a part

35 Initial Report of the United States of America to the United Nations Committee on the Elimination of Racial Discrimination, at 49, delivered to the U.N. Committee on the Elimination of Racial Discrimination (September 2000). http://www.ushrnetwork.org/pubs/CERD.USA.pdf.

36 Kenneth T. Jackson and Ira Katznelson, "When Affirmative Action Was White." In *Crabgrass Frontier* (2005), 115–142. A Report to the U.N. Committee on the Elimination of Racial Discrimination, January 2008. chrome-extension://efaidnbmnnnibpcajpcglclefindmkaj/https://www.prrac.org/pdf/FinalCERDHousingDiscriminationReport.pdf

37 Douglas S. Massey and Nancy A. Denton, *American Apartheid: Segregation and the Making of the Underclass* (Cambridge, MA: Harvard University Press, 1993), 20.

of the problem, by creating isolated, segregated, large-scale public housing neighborhoods. Goering argued that HUD had employed a deliberate policy to locate public housing residents in neighborhoods where their presence would not disturb the prevailing racial pattern. HUD, along with a number of individual local housing authorities, persistently resisted integration, and their policies regarding site selection, tenant selection, and tenant assignment ensured the continuation of racially identifiable public housing in racially concentrated neighborhoods.

Housing policy in the United States has pursued a variety of policy goals that reached well beyond the bounds of shelter. While housing policy can be viewed as social policy, its primary function was seldom the alleviation of poverty. In many ways, federal housing policy has shaped America's cities. The location and quality of government-sponsored housing reflects America's ambivalence toward the poor, and its history mirrors the evolution of American attitudes toward poverty. The fragmented history and purpose of housing policy in the United States demonstrates the importance of recognizing and mitigating the unintended consequences of policy choices.

In *The "Underclass" Debate*, Michael Katz discusses four consequences of federal policies that have shaped the nature of urban poverty in this country: migration, marginalization, exclusion, and isolation. He argued that the massive movement of African Americans into northern cities during the 1940s and 1950s affected housing policy. This migration drastically increased the percentage of blacks living in northern cities that lacked much of the social capital needed to navigate the job market and was more vulnerable to being "trapped" in inner-city neighborhoods, unlike the white populations.[38] Various structures and institutions exacerbated by public policy have kept the poor from moving and have caused stagnation in those neighborhoods. Concurrently, those same policies enabled working and middle-class whites to obtain housing communities far superior to those they left behind in the inner cities. The new suburban communities were quiet, accessible to jobs, and provided superior access to education and city services due to the wealthier tax base.

Katz describes marginalization as the process whereby some combination of factors pushes groups to the edges of the labor force, leaving them

38 Stewart E. Tolnay, Robert M. Adelman, and Kyle D. Crowder, "Race, Regional Origin, and Residence in Northern Cities at the Beginning of the Great Migration." *American Sociological Review* 67, no. 3 (June 2002): 457–458.

redundant, unwanted, or confined to the worst jobs.[39] Because so many of the poor were viewed by mainstream society as outsiders, there was little motivation to provide them with comfort or services. He argued that the portrayal of slum-dwellers as the source of the problems in the inner cities produced a "legitimate" reason to marginalize minority populations. According to Katz, white communities typically received better education, better health, and more reliable transportation than their minority counterparts and federal action in the housing arena through public housing programs exacerbated these differences.

Alexander von Hoffman in "High Ambitions: The Past and Future of American Low-Income Housing Policy," argued that the goal of public housing advocates was to reform and aid the poor by creating a living environment, antithetical to the urban slum, with proper light, heat, and plumbing, but policymakers did not embrace this view, nor did the National Association of Realtors. The opposition, represented by the National Association of Real Estate Brokers (NAREB), argued that public housing would destroy the private housing industry and the self-reliance of tenants.[40]

In Lawrence J. Vale's book, *From the Puritans to the Projects: Public Housing and Public Neighbors*, he discussed how the federal government, local housing authorities, and private organizations such as the NAREB purposefully excluded minorities, single parents, and immigrants from both public housing and the opportunity to purchase homes of their own. In his work, he discussed the Federal Housing Administration policies that were instrumental in providing middle-class families with the means to purchase housing, which also established guidelines to prevent minorities from settling into white neighborhoods that restricted the private sector from investing in inner-city areas. Early federal housing policies focused on rehabilitation, not on aiding the poor or providing services to the poor. Their goal was not only to fix the poor but also to protect mainstream society from their influence, which resulted in a more distinct concentration of poverty.[41] According to Vale, the postwar focus was on the construction of housing and its economic impacts rather than on the needs of the people who needed housing. The majority of federal policy goals concentrated on the community development aspect of

---

39 Michael Katz, *Reframing the Underclass Debate: Views from History* (Princeton, NJ: Princeton University Press, 1993), 452.

40 Norman Krumholtz, "The Reluctant Hand: Privatization of Public Housing in the U.S." Paper presented at the *CITY FUTURES CONFERENCE*, Chicago, July 8–10, 2004.

41 Lawrence J. Vale, *From the Puritans to the Projects: Public Housing and Public Neighbors* (Cambridge, MA: Harvard University Press, 2000).

housing policies; the action taken indicated the federal interest in America's urban poor centered more on the fiscal plight of American cities than on the conditions of the poor themselves.[42]

John Yinger examines housing discrimination and residential segregation in his article "Housing Discrimination and Residential Segregation as Causes of Poverty"; in which he argues that the housing market helps to push people into poverty and to keep them there. He indicated that ethnic discrimination in the housing markets, past and present, magnified these forces for Blacks and Hispanics and therefore helps to explain why people in both groups face higher poverty rates than non-Hispanic Whites.[43] According to Yinger, housing markets contribute to poverty through five channels: high rent burdens, housing health risks, lack of access to housing wealth, neighborhood effects, and spatial mismatch. He suggests that poor people may find it impossible to make the needed investments in health care, education, or job-related expenses, such as child care if they must devote a high share of their income to rent. Consistent with the literature, poor people have settled for poor-quality housing and suffer from housing health risks such as being exposed to lead-based paint and asthma. In Yinger's work, he argued that there are barriers to homeownership (credit constraints, lack of savings) that prevent poor people from gaining access to the most widely used method for obtaining wealth.

Many studies find that growing up in high-poverty neighborhoods influences social and economic outcomes. The outcomes that show up in one or more studies include educational attainment, employment, teenage childbearing, and criminal activity. Various studies find that concentrated poverty has a negative impact on educational performance, which tends to lower a child's performance on standardized tests, lowering their earning potential, and ultimately being in poverty.[44] In *American Apartheid: Segregation and the Making of the Underclass*, Douglas Massey argued that segregation influences poverty in several ways; it interacts with the high poverty rates among Blacks and Hispanics magnifying the disadvantages they face from living in high-poverty neighborhoods.

In the literature, many label public housing as a failure because when established, it was assumed that tenant rents would provide sufficient funding

42 Ibid., 127.

43 Sheldon H. Danziger and Robert H. Haveman, Introduction, *Understanding Poverty* (New York, NY: Russell Sage Foundation, 2001).

44 John Yinger, "Housing Discrimination and Residential Segregation." In *Understanding Poverty*. Edited by Sheldon H. Danziger and Robert H. Haveman (New York, NY: Russell Sage Foundation, 2001).

for maintenance of the projects, which was a significant oversight in the original legislation of the program.[45] However, as the units' aged, and the wealth of the tenants decreased, leaving less money for maintenance just as the buildings required repair.[46] According to Vale, the direct result was the rapid deterioration of many public housing projects during the 1960s, precisely at the time in which the population in the projects became substantially minority. This led to the claim that Blacks were to blame for public housing problems.[47] According to Rosie Tighe, policies that serve to marginalize and isolate the poor ignored the structural causes of poverty in favor of blaming the poor for their own problems.

Housing has been one of the foremost structural forces in determining the spatial, economic, social marginalization, exclusion, and isolation of America's poor.[48] The issue of public housing embodies the ambivalence in America toward aiding the poor. In wanting to emphasize hard work and not giving anyone something for nothing, policymakers have been historically hesitant to pass any legislation concerning the poor and/or their neighborhoods.[49] According to Tighe, housing policy today is increasingly pursued through the tax code and private-sector means, while direct governmental policies have become rare and the governmental action that does exist continues to emphasize goals unrelated to the needs of the poor, focusing instead on the industry, investment, and community development facets of housing.

William J. Wilson proposes a more specific structural model of neighborhood isolation. The resources, welfare culture, and Wilson's models all imply that neighborhoods play an important role in perpetuating poverty and dependency across generations. Wilson claims that the loss of well-paying manufacturing jobs that employed many of the less educated blacks from inner cities and the out-migration of the middle-class blacks from urban poverty areas, together reduced the chances of the remaining impoverished residents and their children from escaping poverty. He argued that the migration of middle-class blacks out of the inner city leaves the poor inner-city residents behind and weakens important socializing institutions such as churches, political machines, and community organizations, which in the past have been supported by middle-class residents and exposed to poverty

---

45 David Listoken, "Federal Housing Policy and Preservation: Historical Evolution, Patterns, and Implications." *Housing Policy Debate* 2, Issue 2 (1991): 163–164.

46 Ibid., 164.

47 Vale, *From the Puritans to the Projects.*

48 Rosie Tighe, "Housing Policy and the Underclass Debate: Policy Choices and Implications (1900–1970)." *Journal of Public Affairs* 18 (Spring 2006): 47–54.

49 Ibid., 53.

area residents, particularly children and teenagers to mainstream alternatives. According to Wilson, middle-class out-migration meant that poverty area residents had few examples of mainstream success, and this limited their expectations about what was possible for them.[50] According to David Ellwood in *Understanding Dependency: Choices, Confidence, or Culture*, inner-city residents are surrounded by failure and come to expect the same. They lose sight of the capacity to pursue mainstream options and job opportunities in the inner city because they have also disappeared.

Welfare Reform

In the literature, if there is one word in the entire area of poverty that arouses controversy, it is the word "welfare." Welfare policy is the slate on which our most trenchant social anxieties are written.[51] Welfare is defined as public programs that give cash payments and non-cash assistance to persons unable to adequately provide for themselves and their families. Charles Murray, in his controversial book, *Losing Ground*, argues that welfare is responsible for perpetuating poverty. According to Murray, welfare has created an underclass, which has become dependent on welfare for generation after generation, especially among blacks. He contends that the welfare underclass is trapped in a vicious cycle of unemployment, under-education, and unwanted pregnancies because its members are content with living off the taxpayers' dollars.

In August 1996, President Bill Clinton signed the Personal Responsibility and Work Opportunity Reconciliation Act (PRWORA), passed by the 104th Congress. The new law abolished the 61-year-old entitlement program, Aid to Families with Dependent Children (AFDC), which was the primary source of cash assistance for poor women with children. In its place, the 1996 legislation created a program organized around block grants given to state governments named Temporary Assistance for Needy Families (TANF). TANF programs no longer represent a federal entitlement; it leaves states with the sole discretion in determining eligibility. Under the new welfare system, states have gained more control over program rules; time limits on the receipt of aid; rules and benefits designed to promote work and tougher requirements for program participation; and penalties for noncompliance.

In the article, "Ghettos, Fiscal Federalism, and Welfare Reform," Michael K. Brown argued that welfare reform in 1996 had little to do with poverty and a lot to do with racialized politics of poverty. Conservatives declared that

50 Corcoran, "Rags to Rags," 245.

51 Burton, *The Poverty Debate*, 71.

anything was better than the old welfare system for poor women, and the new plan, with tough work requirements and time-limit benefits was a policy of hope. According to Brown, the conservatives were interested in politically exploiting the issue and describing the Democrats as defenders of "amoral" black women in ghettos.[52] Liberals rationalized welfare reform as necessary, but they also understood it to be a way of banishing race, and racialized poverty, from political lexicon.[53] For the Democrats, welfare reform was as much about solving their frayed relationship with disgruntled, irate middle-class voters as it was about poverty. The debate over the passage of the 1996 law assumed that the persistence of racialized poverty (African American and Latino poverty rates are greater than those of whites) was rooted in the individual failure by and large, the failure of poor blacks to accept work when it was available, a failure to stay in school, or a refusal to get married.[54] Liberals accepted the need for work and self-discipline; but also acknowledged the massive decline in good jobs in big cities was the main cause of urban poverty. Michael K. Brown argued that the problem with governmental policy was not that it had been too generous, or that it contributed to the bad behavior of poor women, but rather, it has always been insufficient.

Throughout the literature, many agree that the welfare system defies American values that stress work and self-sufficiency and believe that it is unfair to the working families who survive on low wages without government assistance.[55] Consequently, state cash assistance programs are now oriented toward work, and a large proportion of recipients receiving cash assistance is required to prepare for work and seek employment.[56] The problem is that large amounts of TANF recipients experience "barriers to employment" and their circumstances make it more difficult or close to impossible for them to find and maintain a job.[57] Still, recipients are faced with several barriers to employment such as mental health issues, a low level of skills, domestic violence, limited English proficiency, lack of transportation, unaffordable

52 Michael K. Brown, "Ghettos, Fiscal Federalism, and Welfare Reform." In *Race and the Politics of Welfare Reform.* Edited by Sanford F. Schram, Joe Soss, and Richard C. Fording (Ann Arbor, MI: The University of Michigan Press, 2003), 47.

53 Ibid.

54 Ibid., 49.

55 Mary B. Larner, Donna L. Terman, and Richard E. Behrman, "The Future of the Children." *Welfare to Work* 7 (Spring 1997): 4.

56 Sharon Parrott, "Welfare Recipients Who Find Jobs: What Do We Know About Their Employment Earnings?" *Center on Budget and Policy Priorities* (November 1998). www.cbpp.org.

57 Economic Issue Guide: Frequently Asked Questions. www.epinet.org.

childcare, as well as inadequate housing.[58] According to Heidi Goldberg, several organizations have completed studies on the prevalence of barriers to employment among TANF recipients. A study by Manpower Demonstrations and Research Corporation reported that 32 percent of non-employed TANF recipients reported fair or poor health. The Urban Institute found that 44 percent of the adults who received assistance in 1999 did not have a GED or a high school diploma. Between 15–30 percent were victims of domestic violence, and between 50–65 percent have been victims at some time during their lives. Many welfare recipients experience more than one barrier toward employment; they also face compounding challenges in securing employment.[59] According to Sharon Parrott, the jobs held by parents that have left welfare or who are combining work and assistance face barriers, which often fail to provide basic health benefits (paid sick leave or vacation time); are paid less than $8.00 per hour, and a substantial portion earn less than $6.00 per hour; and despite the relatively high number of weekly work hours, recipients who do find jobs typically earn between $2,000 and $2,700 per quarter, a total well below the poverty line for a family of three.[60] Although many states have freed up resources, recipients who find jobs will continue to struggle and are much more likely to have incomes that are inadequate to meet their families' basic needs.

Some have argued that the welfare reform successes to date prove that the law is working and should be renewed with only minor adjustments such as cutting funding. Others disagree because families that have left welfare are continuously struggling to make ends meet and those who are approaching welfare time limits are not equipped to enter the workforce.[61] For many years, liberals have advocated that increasing welfare benefits is the best way to reduce poverty, especially among single parents. Many liberals remain concerned and believe that the welfare reform law of 1996, which requires work, encourages marriage along with time-limit benefits, would have adverse consequences on the poor.[62] In the literature on welfare reform, marriage promotion programs have received considerable criticism. The law suggests that moms on welfare should just find themselves a good man (who makes a good

58 Ibid., 2.

59 Ibid., 3.

60 Parrott, "Welfare Recipients Who Find Jobs."

61 Debating Welfare Reform: What's Happened? What's Next? Welfare, U.S. Poverty, Children & Families, Cities. http://www.brookings.edu/events/2001/0220welfare.aspx.

62 Isabel V. Sawhill, "Senior Fellow, Economic Studies Ron Haskins, Senior Fellow, Economic Studies." http://www.brookings.edu/papers/2003/09childrenfamilies.

salary) to solve all of their problems.[63] The welfare reform bill encourages that women should be economically dependent on a man. Some think this increases the possibility that women will not be able to leave the marriage if it is abusive. Others believe that marriage promotion programs suggest that women are incapable of working and raising their children without a man.[64] Opponents suggest that more child support money should be given to the single parent, but many states usually keep child support money to pay back the TANF costs. Many propose that this practice keeps TANF recipients in poverty. Alternatively, others would like for the government to cut back on social welfare spending, moving individuals off the system and placing them into jobs. Welfare reform has hindered many of those individuals who left welfare for the workforce, which has left them trapped in poverty. In the book titled *The Politics of Welfare Reform*, Lyke Thompson and Donald F. Norris argue that welfare is an inadequate response to the poverty problem; it is perceived to neither increase income enough neither to end poverty nor to encourage its recipients to stand up and leave it on their own. During the 1960s major expansions in the size of grants and the range of services took place through Lyndon B. Johnson's Great Society programs. Lyndon B. Johnson's Great Society programs sought to change the basic institutional structures and environmental conditions that created poverty. Although his efforts were high and created many new programs that helped the poor serve some purpose, at the end of the decade, poverty was far from being eliminated.[65] According to Thompson and Norris, the partial failure of the Great Society programs and antipoverty policies demoralized many liberals who had expected more, helping to open the door for more conservative approaches.

The majority of the literature on poverty has been studied, argued, and established on the assumptions rooted in a substantial body of research that involves the "culture of poverty" debate of the 1960s. These arguments assume that the poor have distinct values, aspirations, and psychological characteristics, which inhibit their achievement and produce behavioral deviancies that will keep them poor and persist not only within but also across generations through socialization of the young.[66] Consequently, these

63 http://www.womenmatter.com/womrights_lifeissues.htm#Wel.

64 http://www.womenmatter.com.

65 Lyke Thompson and Donald F. Norris, *The Politics of Welfare Reform* (Thousand Oaks, CA: Sage Publications, Inc., 1995), 5.

66 Mary Corcoran, Greg J. Duncan, Gerald Gurin, and Patricia Gurin, "Myth and Reality: The Causes and Persistence of Poverty." *Journal of Policy Analysis and Management* 4, no. 4 (Summer 1985): 517. http://www.jstor.org/stable/3323752 (Accessed May 02, 2011).

arguments have implications for poverty policies. If poverty and dependency are culturally and psychologically rooted, then poverty can never be eliminated simply by providing economic resources and opportunities.[67] The majority of the arguments presented here refer to the culture of poverty theories and blaming the victim approaches, which are generally inappropriate models for viewing the poor and are seen as a major weakness in the literature. Another weakness in the literature is that today's critics are saying very little that is new, and their current attacks on the poor and the programs established to help them replicate many responses expressed during the nineteenth century. Further research is needed and must begin with scholars researching and challenging the entire governmental system, its structures, and policies that were implemented based on fixed preconceived notions and ideologies about servicing the poor.

Researching the persistent poverty among African Americans in the United States is necessary because it will reconceptualize poverty, present a paradigm shift, and transform (restructure) public policy in a dramatic way. This research is useful because it will change the way the public, scholars, and policymakers view the poor. This research is valid because it focuses on the entire governmental system, unlike the previous and present governmental systems that rest solely on the explicit or implicit assumptions regarding and/or blaming the individual. The most comprehensive studies that have been put forth to date have been consistent with the culture of poverty theory from proponents such as Michael Harrington, Oscar Lewis, Walter Miller, and Edward Banfield, just to name a few. There has been an ongoing debate between the conservatives and liberals on the causes and explanations of poverty and how to solve those problems. There have been no new developments offered in the literature, only expansions to the literature, which offer the same prescriptions. Previous research has suggested that the system is to blame for the poverty that exists in the United States among minority groups, but it has been ignored or discredited because it's not in line with the dominant ideology and this has created a gap in the literature on poverty. This scholarship will fill the gap in the literature because it has challenged the entire governmental system, its structure, and policies, while reshaping the United States' public policies and views about the poor. This scholarship offers guidelines for policymakers to follow new policy initiatives and recommendations for future research.

67 Ibid.

Chapter 3

HISTORY AND RESPONSES TO THE WAR ON POVERTY ANTI-POVERTY POLICIES

President Lyndon B. Johnson assumed office in November 1963, after John F. Kennedy's assassination. Johnson declared an unconditional war on poverty in 1964, which was based on Kennedy's domestic programs, called The New Frontier that promised to outlaw segregation in federally supported housing (but not much else for civil rights), a higher minimum wage, federal aid for low-income housing and education, and hospital insurance for retirees.[1] Lyndon B. Johnson agreed to tackle the poverty problem because it was an issue that was close to his heart. Having grown up in poverty and working during his adult life on policies that expanded opportunities, Johnson was eager to assist poor Americans he recognized the great need in America, making the anti-poverty programs his number one legislative priority.[2] The anti-poverty programs of the War on Poverty went to Congress and were signed into law on August 20, 1964, which created a new agency, the Office of Economic Opportunity (OEO).

Congress and President Kennedy quickly implemented three initiatives that prefigured the War on Poverty. The first consisted of efforts to reform welfare. In 1962, the Kennedy administration won congressional approval for public welfare amendments that increased federal funding for training social workers and expanding services to recipients.[3] The amendments were aimed to get people off welfare by encouraging and fostering conventional families and jobs; the method used would be intensive casework that involved

---

1 Frank Stricker, *Why America Lost The War On Poverty – And How To Win It* (Chapel Hill, NC: The University of North Carolina Press, 2007), 37.

2 Janine Heiser, "Lyndon B. Johnson's Power Prospects Strategy: The Case of the War on Poverty." Oberlin College. http://www.thepresidency.org/storage/documents/Calkins/Heiser.pdf.

3 Stricker, *Why America Lost The War On Poverty*, 38.

counseling for self-esteem and life skills that might include job training and job placement. The people who planned the War on Poverty forged ahead with the same old conventional assumptions that the poor needed services and personal rehabilitation rather than a federal jobs program and more money.[4] The second initiative was another program that linked concerns about structural unemployment and poverty. On May 1, 1961, Congress passed the Redevelopment Act, and as a result, depressed mining, textile, railroad, and fishing communities could apply for grants and loans to improve public facilities and attract new businesses.[5] The third initiative that prefigured the War on Poverty was the Manpower Development and Training Act (MDTA) of March 25, 1962. The notion behind this Act was the belief that rapid technological change, often called "automation" was pushing well-paid workers out of jobs and into poverty, eventually becoming a program for the poor and disadvantaged.[6]

Many occurrences led to a War on Poverty such as, concerns about welfare dependency; the absence of strong economic growth from 1958 to 1962; foundations and community activists were analyzing urban decay and urban renewal; and juvenile delinquency provoked discussion, as did the problems of depressed areas.[7] According to Frank Stricker, liberals and unionist worried about the automation of unemployment, the MDTA, which had been enacted to provide job retraining, was running out of experienced older workers and becoming a war on poverty for the hard-core (young, inner-city, black males) unemployed. There were also factors that created a context for the War on Poverty such as, America's confidence that it could solve the poverty problem and the role of the civil rights movement.

Social scientists Frances Fox Piven and Richard Cloward argued that the War on Poverty was a part of a presidential electoral strategy to calm protest and win black votes, but some anti-poverty planners denied that civil rights activism catalyzed the War on Poverty. In 1963, Kennedy began to think seriously about civil rights; he learned that low incomes were a crucial part of the poverty problem.[8] Lyndon Johnson sometimes conceived the War on Poverty as a device to get money and services to blacks without arousing the white sentiment of the South. Furthermore, the daily headlines about

---

4 Gertrude Schaffner Goldberg and Shelia D. Collins, *Washington' New Poor Law: Welfare Reform and the Roads Not Taken 1935 – Present* (New York, NY: Apex Press, 2000), 75–78.

5 Stricker, *Why America Lost The War On Poverty*, 38.

6 Ibid., 39.

7 Ibid., 41.

8 Ibid.

economic discrimination and the demonstrations made the anti-poverty effort seem urgent.[9]

The War on Poverty would not mainly be a jobs or income program; it would be an experiment in training, education, and motivational rehabilitation for a relatively small group of individuals outside the regular economy. In the 1964 Economic Report to the President, his economist used the culture of poverty theory to describe a vicious cycle, stating that "poverty breeds poverty; lacks motivation, hope, and incentive, which is a less powerful barrier than the lack of financial means." Frank Stricker argued that the War on Poverty was the culture of poverty in the service of liberal anti-poverty programs that would not challenge the privileges of the very rich or corporate America.

The War on Poverty created several new programs including Medicare and Medicaid, Model Cities, the Elementary and Secondary Education Act (ESEA), Higher Education Act (HEA) and Job Opportunities in the Business Sector (JOBS). Johnson also expanded and improved existing programs such as, food stamps, welfare, and Social Security. The Great Society legislation was viewed as the government providing a hand up, not a handout. The basis was a thriving economy (which the 1964 tax cut sparked) in such circumstances, that most Americans would be able to enjoy the material blessings of society. Consequently, others would need help and support with health care, education, training, housing, and a nondiscriminatory try at employment, to share in the nation's wealth. Johnson was through with his actions; he created a vast empire of laws and agencies called the Great Society that targeted everything from highway safety to improving the arts and humanities, from expanding the welfare state with new programs like Medicare and Medicaid to improving old programs like Social Security. Above all, he was the first American president thoroughly committed to providing civil rights for African Americans.[10]

Anti-Poverty Programs/Policies

The objective of the Economic Opportunity Act of 1964 was to further United States policy in eliminating "the paradox of poverty in the midst of plenty," by opening an opportunity to everyone in education and training, the opportunity to equal employment and the opportunity to live in decency

9 Ibid.
10 Ibid., 50.

and with dignity.[11] One of the main purposes of the Economic Opportunity Act was to provide comprehensive action and coordination against poverty. Its emphasis was on local initiative and voluntary action, supported by federal funding covering 90 percent or even 100 percent of project costs. The principle objective of the Economic Opportunity Act was to create opportunities for the impoverished to help themselves.[12] The major influence of the Economic Opportunity Act was the Community Action Programs (CAP). The objectives of the CAPs were to call upon the huge collection of local initiatives, to fill the gaps of existing programs and to provide mechanisms for coordinated local planning and action. A CAP is a program that is operated in any urban or rural area including a state, metropolitan area, county, city, and town multi-city unit. It provides services, assistance, and other activities of sufficient scope and size that grant promises toward the elimination and causes of poverty; it is developed and administered with participation from community residents or group members being served; and it is conducted, administered, or coordinated by a public or nonprofit agency.[13]

This chapter assess the programs that were usually associated with the War on Poverty, those that were run by the OEO. In particular, this chapter will review the anti-poverty programs that offer people education, training, housing, health, and social welfare. An essential part of the War on Poverty was job training. The poor had less education and less training than the non-poor, and the anti-poverty planners thought that if poor people had the right skills they would get good jobs and rise out of poverty.

Manpower Development Training Act

The Manpower Development and Training Act (MDTA) was signed into law by President Kennedy in 1962 two years before the War on Poverty. It grew out of concern in the late 1950s that technological unemployment was worsening. The MDTA spent $1.5 billion in six years, and as the economic growth picked up, many displaced workers found jobs; MDTA served the newly jobless and poor young people.[14] According to Mangum and Walsh, within six years, 600,000 Americans completed an MDTA course. Some

11 Economic Opportunity Act of 1964. 2,278Stat. 508, 42 U.S.C 2701 (1964).

12 Michael S. March, "Coordination of the War on Poverty." In *Anti-Poverty Programs.* Edited by Robinson O. Everett (Dobbs Ferry, NY: Oceana Publications, Inc., 1966), 139.

13 Sec. 202, 78 Stat. 516, 42 U.S.C 2782 (1964).

14 Allen J. Matusow, *The Unraveling of America: A History of Liberalism in the 1960's* (New York, NY: Harper Torchbooks, 1984), 104.

studies showed that graduates improved annual earnings by $1,000 or more; others found a gain of only $269. Because few evaluations included control groups, it was impossible to tell how the same types of people were doing without the MDTA.[15] The overall conclusion came from two students of the MDTA: "After 10 years, there is still no definitive evidence one way or the other about MDTA outcomes."[16] Some MDTA training programs were poorly run, and students had weak educational backgrounds or drug problems. The MDTA was fundamentally flawed, because it was based on the theory of structural unemployment: people were jobless and poor because they lacked the skills to take existing jobs; and the MDTA did not create jobs; instead, it increased the number of people applying for jobs.[17] Greenleigh Associates argued that unless there were significant job shortages for which the poor could be trained, anti-poverty training programs might not lower poverty rates.

Youth Training Programs

A second prominent training program of the War on Poverty focused on the young. Title I of the Economic Opportunity Act created the Job Corps to remove young people (16–21) from the harmful effects of their communities and teach them school subjects, good job habits, and to train them in welding, auto repair, and other blue-collar trades.[18] The initial proposal for the Job Corps applied only to young men, but after women in Congress protested, Job Corps was opened to women. Anti-poverty planners assumed that more education meant less poverty.

The Neighborhood Youth Corps offered part-time summer work in landscaping, painting parking meters, and clean-up jobs to low-income youths who stayed in school. Upward-Bound programs offered summer programs to high school juniors and seniors to enrich their cultural experience and to help them succeed in college.[19] In favor of low-income college students there

---

15 Garth L. Magnum and John Walsh, *A Decade of Manpower Development Training* (Salt Lake City, UT: Olympus Publishing Co., 1973), 22–35, 41–44.

16 Ibid., 44.

17 Henry M. Levin, "A Decade of Policy Developments in Improving Education and Training for Low-Income Populations." In *A Decade of Federal Antipoverty Programs: Achievements, Failures, and Lessons.* Edited by Robert H. Haveman (New York, NY: Academic Press, 1977), 179.

18 Irwin Unger, *The Best of Intentions: The Triumph and Failures of the Great Society Under Kennedy, Johnson, and Nixon* (Chicago, IL: Doubleday Press, 1996), 179, 183.

19 Ibid., 183.

were grants, loans, and jobs, including the Work-Study Program, in which the federal government paid 90 percent of the wages for up to 15 hours a week for full-time college students in good standing; almost 400,000 students were soon involved in this program.[20]

According to Unger, on the physical side the Job Corps worked, trainees gained weight, a third were fitted for glasses, and many received dental services, but generally the results were not good: two-thirds of Job Corps enrollees never finished the course, and graduates earned wages that were the same as no-shows who had been accepted to the program but never entered. In the Congressional Record in 1967, critics claimed that the costs of educating a student in Job Corps were as much as sending someone to Harvard.[21] In fact, the Job Corps tried something more difficult than educating a Harvard student and it was handicapped by the missing link to good jobs.[22] According to Stricker, this was the downfall of anti-poverty programs, it may have been a good idea to modernize young people from low-income families to improve their schooling, polish them up for the job market, and address their health needs, but many trainees already had middle-class aspirations; and if job offers did not follow, they would grow more cynical.

Head Start Anti-poverty Program

The branch of the OEO that won the most political support was the Head Start Program. Half of the nation's poor were children; anti-poverty planners assumed that early intervention might break the cycle of poverty that perpetuates itself year after year. Head Start was a preschool enrichment program that offset cultural deprivation, and the negative influence of low-income families and communities.[23] The Head Start program was created as a national child development program for children from birth to age five. Head Start was designed to provide comprehensive school readiness, and enhance a child's physical, social, emotional and cognitive development, which enabled parents to become better caregivers and teachers to their children, as well as to meet their own goals of economic independence. The guiding philosophy of the Head Start program was to invest now, and benefit later, which was based on the belief that high-quality early childhood care, education and

20 Sar A. Levitan, *The Great Society's Poor Law* (Baltimore, MD: Johns Hopkins Press, 1969), 173.

21 Ibid., 171–172.

22 Stricker, *Why America Lost The War On Poverty*, 65.

23 Edward Zigler and Susan Muenchow, *Head Start: The Inside Story of America's Most Successful Educational Experiment* (New York, NY: Basic Books, 1992), 3.

family services promote success and will pay off with a multitude of benefits, to children, their families, and society as a whole.

In 1968, Head Start received tremendous support, becoming a full-year program serving 218,000 children.[24] According to Zigler and Muenchow, no matter how successful Head Start was, it was underfunded; its staff was paid poorly; and it could not revolutionize the class structure or create good permanent jobs for Head Start graduates. Zigler and Muenchow argued that it was not the poor who failed, but the federal government and some federal programs that caused more poverty.

Medicare and Medicaid

During the spring of 1964, Lyndon B. Johnson began to use the term "Great Society" to describe his reform programs, and that term described his most notable anti-poverty policies and CAPs. Under Johnson's leadership, the passage of Medicare, a health insurance program for the elderly, and Medicaid, a program providing health-care assistance for the poor, was enacted and the federal government assumed major responsibility for the funding of health care. On July 30, 1965, President Johnson signed into law the Health Insurance for the Aged Act—Medicare.[25] Medicare is a near-universal program that covers the elderly regardless of income. The original bill provides all persons aged 65 years and older with a basic health insurance plan consisting of inpatient hospital services, post-hospital care, outpatient diagnostic services, and home health care visits, subject to certain coinsurance and deductibles financed by a payroll tax.[26] For the same population, the bill authorized a voluntary supplementary medical insurance (SMI) plan covering physicians' services such as X-rays and laboratory tests, which was financed by a three-dollar monthly premium paid by each enrollee and a matching general fund paid by the federal government.[27] In the first year of the program's enactment, 19.1 million elderly were covered under the basic plan and 17.1 million had enrolled in the SMI program.[28] The negative aspect of Medicare is the growth in the amount of coinsurance and deductibles placed on the low-income elderly. However, Medicare has kept near-poor elderly Americans out of poverty and has eased

24 Ibid., 28.

25 Karen Davis, "A Decade of Policy Developments in Providing Health Care for Low-Income Families." In *A Decade of Federal Antipoverty Programs: Achievements, Failures, and Lessons*. Edited by Robert H. Haveman (New York, NY: Academic Press, 1977), 79.

26 Ibid., 80.

27 Ibid.

28 Ibid.

the anxieties of elderly persons whose life savings would have been wiped out because of a major illness.[29] The anti-poverty significance of Medicare was its availability to the aged and some of the disabled; even though it lacked provision for dental care and prescription drugs, it kept elderly individuals' health costs from absorbing major portions of their income.

Along with Medicare, Medicaid was also signed into law on July 30, 1965. Medicaid provides health-care coverage to many, but by no means to all of the poor. Eligibility is determined, to a substantial degree, by the states, which provide a large proportion of Medicaid funding. In general, all members of families who receive public assistance through ADFC/TANF, SSI, and Social Security Disability programs, are eligible for those programs covered by Medicaid even if they do not receive benefits from them.[30] In 1963, most elderly Americans had no health insurance and few retirement plans provided such coverage. The poor had little access to medical treatment until they were in critical condition; only wealthier Americans could get the finest care, and only by traveling to a few big cities like Boston or New York.

Joseph Califano in "What Was Really Great About the War on Poverty: The Truth Behind Conservative Myths," states that Medicare and Medicaid programs have worked. His study illustrates that since 1965, 79 million Americans have signed up for Medicare; since 1966, Medicaid has served more than 200 million needy Americans; and in 1967, two years after its enactment it served 10 million poor citizens and in 1997, 39 million.[31] The 1968 heart, cancer, and stroke legislation provided funds to staff and created centers of medical excellence throughout major cities. The 1965 Health Professions Educational Assistance Act provided resources to double the number of doctors graduating from medical schools, from 8,000 to 16,000.[32] That Act also increased the pool of specialists and researchers, nurses, and paramedics. Community health centers were also a part of the Great Society health-care agenda, and today they serve almost 8 million Americans annually. The Great Society's commitment to fund basic medical research lifted the National Institutes of Health to unprecedented financial heights, starting a harvest of medical miracles.[33]

29 Sar A. Levitan, Garth L. Mangum, Stephen L. Mangum, and Andrew Sum, *Programs in Aid of the Poor* (Baltimore, MD: The Johns Hopkins University Press, 2003), 91.

30 Ibid.

31 Joseph A. Califano, "What Was Really Great About the War on Poverty: The Truth Behind the Conservative Myths." *Washington Monthly*, 1999. http://www.washingtonmonthly.com/features/1999/9910.califano.html#byline.

32 Ibid.

33 Ibid.

Herbert E. Klarman argued that the health-care programs were quite different from what was originally anticipated: the cost of Medicare and Medicaid quickly surpassed original estimates; rapid increases in medical care costs, particularly for hospital care medical expenditures; the rapid growth in welfare rolls increased the cost of the Medicaid program, placing strains on both state and federal budgets. According to Karen Davis, the unanticipated high cost of medical care financing programs led to widespread dissatisfaction and seriously undermined the attempt to provide high-quality health care to the poor. As a result, state governments reduced their budgets by cutting benefits, reimbursements levels to providers of medical services, and where possible, tightening eligibility requirements.[34]

These actions contributed to the inability of the program to live up to the high expectations of those low-income persons hoping to receive high-quality medical care and of those hoping to receive compensation for providing such care.[35] However, providing health care services to poor and elderly individuals have made remarkable gains such as having access to medical care services, experimental health delivery programs, improving the health of the poor, and overcoming a multitude of obstacles.

Medicaid appears to have been instrumental improving the impoverished access to medical care but the poor still does not participate in mainstream medicine of comparable quality, convenience, and style that's received by non-poor persons. The poor continue to receive care in crowded dreary clinics with longer waits and few amenities.[36] The enactment of Medicare and Medicaid has allowed African Americans access to medical care but some segments of the African American population continuously lack coverage. The U.S. Census Bureau reports that in 2009, (21.0) percent of African Americans were uninsured, compared to (13.2) of whites that were not covered. The percentage of people covered by government health insurance programs increased to (29.0) percent in 2009 from (27.8) in 2007.[37] The percentage and number of people covered by Medicaid increased to (14.3) percent in 2009, from (13.2) percent in 2007, (27.1) percent were African Americans, and (9.8) were white Americans. The percentage and number of people covered by

34 Davis, "A Decade of Policy Developments in Providing Health Care for Low-Income Families," 198.

35 Ibid.

36 Ibid., 204.

37 United States Census Bureau. "Health Insurance Coverage Status and Type of Coverage - All Persons by Sex, Race and Hispanic Origin 1999 to 2009." Health Insurance Historical Tables. www.census.gov.

Medicare in 2009 (14.3), which was not statistically different from 2008, (11.9) are African Americans (Table 3.1), and (15.4) are whites.[38]

Elementary and Secondary Education Act of 1965

Congress enacted the ESEA of 1965 Public Law 80-10, on April 9, 1965. It was the primary vehicle for the federal government to strengthen and improve educational quality and educational opportunities in the nations' elementary and secondary schools. Financial assistance was given to local educational agencies for the education of children in low-income families. Title I of the ESEA of 1965, provided financial assistance for local agencies in areas affected by government action. The ESEA placed an emphasis on equal access to education, which established high standards and accountability from state and local governments. The law authorized federally funded educational programs that were administered by the states, which encouraged state governments to become more involved in education.

Higher Education Act of 1965

On November 8, 1965, Congress enacted the HEA of 1965 Public Law 89-329 to strengthen the educational resources of United States' colleges and universities and to provide financial assistance to students for post-secondary and higher education. Title IV of the HEA of 1965, authorized educational opportunity grants for students with exceptional financial need.[39] HEA was one of the most important pieces of Great Society legislation. According to historian Robert Dallek, Johnson had an "almost mystical faith" in the capacity of education to transform people's lives. President Roosevelt viewed social help in terms of putting money into people's pockets, but Johnson believed in enabling people to solve their problems through education.[40] One of his highest Great Society priorities was to broaden educational opportunities for all Americans, and the chief legislative instruments for doing so were the ESEA for elementary and secondary students and the HEA for postsecondary students. Johnson hoped the HEA would help every willing individual to receive a postsecondary education that would lead to a higher income for the individual and/or their

---

38 Ibid.

39 Laurence E. Lynn, "Policy Developments in Income Maintenance System." In *A Decade of Federal Antipoverty Programs: Achievements, Failures, and Lessons*. Edited by Robert H. Haveman (New York, NY: Academic Press, 1977), 81.

40 The Wayne Morse Youth Program. http://www.waynemorsenow.org.

Table 3.1 Health coverage status and type of coverage by race, 1999–2009.

Year	*Total People Percentages*	*Private Health Insurance Total*	*Employment-Based*	*Direct Purchase*	*Government Health Insurance Total*	*Medicaid*	*Medicare*	*Military*	*Not Covered*
White Americans									
2009	100.0	72.7	63.3	10.6	26.8	9.8	15.4	5.1	13.2
2008	100.0	74.8	65.7	10.2	25.5	8.8	15.2	4.7	12.0
2007	100.0	76.0	66.8	10.3	24.7	8.4	14.6	4.5	11.3
2006	100.0	76.3	67.1	10.4	24.0	8.3	14.4	4.4	12.0
2005	100.0	76.2	67.3	10.2	24.2	8.2	14.5	4.6	11.8
2004	100.0	76.4	67.1	10.5	24.4	8.3	14.6	4.5	11.7
2003	100.0	77.1	68.1	10.4	23.6	7.7	14.5	4.3	11.4
2002	100.0	78.1	69.2	10.5	22.6	6.9	14.0	4.2	11.2
African Americans									
2009	100.0	48.7	44.7	4.5	38.9	27.1	11.9	4.0	21.0
2008	100.0	52.2	48.2	4.3	37.2	25.4	11.9	4.1	19.1
2007	100.0	53.4	49.0	4.5	35.0	23.8	11.4	3.6	19.5
2006	100.0	53.6	49.2	4.7	33.3	22.8	10.9	3.3	20.5
2005	100.0	54.0	49.4	5.2	35.6	24.8	11.1	3.7	19.0
2004	100.0	54.4	50.2	4.9	35.6	24.8	10.7	3.9	18.8
2003	100.0	54.1	50.2	4.7	34.8	24.4	11.0	3.4	19.1
2002	100.0	54.6	50.8	4.4	33.7	23.1	10.5	3.5	19.7

Source: United States Census Bureau, Current Population Survey, Annual Social and Economic Supplements

families. In addition to, decreasing the poverty of individuals, Johnson also believed that additional and higher-quality education would benefit the country by ensuring a steady supply of educated individuals that will provide the human resources needed for economic prosperity.[41]

In American society, education has traditionally been viewed as crucial to the achievement of upward economic mobility. Free public education at elementary and secondary levels has served as one of the most important symbols of society's commitment to equal opportunity. Michael Morris and John B. Williamson argued that it is highly unlikely for educational interventions to reduce poverty to the extent implied by America's equality of opportunity ideology. Sociologists have argued that education has a relatively powerful role in explaining social mobility among individuals, and economists have viewed education as an investment in human capital that raises the productivity and incomes of individuals.[42] Arthur Mann argued that education prevents poverty. According to Morris and Williamson, no matter how much policymakers and the public may wish otherwise, the ability of most of the aforementioned approaches to reduce or eliminate poverty is severely constrained because it assumes that the individual is to blame, and refuse to look at the governmental system or its economic and political structures.

Food Stamp Act of 1965

The Food Stamp Act of 1965 (P.L. 88-525) authorized a food stamp program, which allowed low-income households to receive a greater share of the nation's food abundance; it was designed to safeguard the health and well-being of the population; and to raise levels of nutrition among low-income families. The goal of the Food Stamp program was to prevent hunger, improve the social conditions among citizens with low-income and to provide a foundation for United States agriculture. The available evidence indicates that food stamps are more effective as a public assistance program than as a food and nutrition program. Critics of the Food Stamp program frequently emphasize the fact that most participants end up spending a little more for food than they would have if they had simply received the cash equivalent of the stamps.[43] Moreover, because the stamps can be used to purchase just about any type of food, the program provides recipients with little incentive to upgrade the

---

41 Joseph Califano, "What was Really Great about the Great Society?" *The Washington Monthly Online*. http://www.washingtonmonthly.com (Accessed February 10, 2011).

42 Levin, "A Decade of Policy Developments in Improving Education and Training for Low-Income Populations," 123.

43 Michael Morris and John B. Williamson, *Poverty and Policy: An Analysis of Federal Intervention Efforts* (Westport, CT: Greenwood Press, 1986), 97.

basic nutritional quality of their diets.[44] The improvement that has occurred appears to be mainly due to the fact that stamps enable the poor to buy more, rather than, better food.[45]

Housing and Urban Development Act of 1965

The Housing and Urban Development Act of 1965 (P.L. 89-117, 79) extended the urban renewal programs set in motion by the 1949 act, which provided various forms of federal assistance to cities for removing dilapidated housing and redeveloping parts of downtowns. The act also extended the code enforcement program, which required that cities enact a code specifying minimum standards for housing before they could participate in the urban renewal program. In addition, HUD extended Federal Housing Administration mortgage-insurance programs, which enabled more American families to purchase a home. The basis for the act is Congress's taxing and spending power as stated in the U.S. Constitution, article I, section 8, which authorizes the legislature to provide for the general welfare.

The most controversial and innovative part of the act, however, created a rent-supplement program. Under this program, qualified tenants paid 25 percent of their income in rent, and the program paid the balance directly to the housing provider. The rent supplement ceased when the occupant was able to pay the full rent. To qualify, a person's income had to be within the limits set for eligibility for public housing, and the person had to be either elderly, physically handicapped, displaced by a public-improvement program, living in substandard housing, or occupying housing damaged by a natural disaster. Only private, nonprofit corporations were eligible housing sponsors. Many inner-city housing authorities were unable to maintain their existing units in the face of such widespread problems, which led to public opposition that frequently forestalled the initiation of new projects.[46] Rising construction and operating costs further undermined political support for public housing, which led to a decline in federal funding and the number of units decreasing.[47] Housing does not lend itself to insurance, but at existing costs, the poor cannot adequately house themselves, especially to the extent necessary for the well-being of their children.[48]

44 Ibid.

45 Ibid., 98.

46 Levitan, Mangum, Mangum, and Sum, *Programs in Aid of the Poor*, 105.

47 Ibid.

48 Ibid., 128.

Chapter 4

POLICY ANALYSIS AND FINDINGS

This chapter focuses on the results of the policy analysis of Lyndon B. Johnson's War on Poverty anti-poverty policies. Lyndon B. Johnson oversold and underfinanced the War on Poverty. Worse, the war was conceptually flawed. Johnson and anti-poverty planners censored alternative approaches. Although notable in their thinking about poverty, was the absence of any mention of the economic system within which it operated.[1] The anti-poverty programs targeted the poorest of the poor and segregated them from the larger population that also faced economic risk on a daily basis. The successes of the War on Poverty remain controversial. Ronald Reagan asserted a decade later that the government had declared a war on poverty and poverty had won. Conservatives claimed that the real victories against poverty stemmed from individual willpower and economic growth, not government programs.[2] Michael Harrington suggests that because of the war in Vietnam, the War on Poverty programs were underfunded and never given a chance. Others, like political scientist John Schwarz, concluded that cash programs such as Social Security and welfare, not economic growth and training programs, produced most of the 1960s success against poverty.[3] Historian, Irwin Unger, claims that anything other than what the Johnson administration did was impossibly utopian. However, there was nothing as utopian as programs that led to nowhere; the poor learned that once the training was over, there was no job. Survey data showed that Americans would have supported other approaches; and the War on Poverty could have emphasized government job creation or better income policies. Johnson and his economic advisors were at fault; their political caution and constricted ideology did not want the social programs

1 Frank Stricker, *Why America Lost the War on Poverty – And How To Win It* (Chapel Hill, NC: The University of North Carolina Press, 2007), 80.

2 Ibid., 61.

3 Michael Harrington, *The New American Poverty* (New York, NY: Penguin Books, 1985), 21.

to threaten the middle-class pocketbooks or business power.[4] A great deal was done, but the War on Poverty itself failed to solve poverty; it focused on the very poor and did not deal with the income and employment problems of average working-class families. So, these families felt that their problems were being ignored, especially when it appeared that the poor were black and the working class was white. The anti-poverty crusade did not conquer poverty, but it provided weapons to the enemies of liberalism.

The War on Poverty programs began too hastily, expanded too rapidly, wasted too much money, and promised more than it could deliver. More adequate planning and small-scale demonstration projects would have been valuable, from a programmatic perspective.[5] The inflated pronouncements of the War on Poverty caused expectations that were impossibly high and the anti-poverty rhetoric helped to awaken the public to the problem of poverty. As an operating agency, the Office of Economic Opportunity failed to coordinate a government-wide effort, but it did succeed in focusing the government's attention toward the poor. Indeed, the impact of the poverty programs on people's lives, and on government at all levels, has been profound. According to Harding, the war in Vietnam meant military spending and inadequate funding for the anti-poverty programs.

Educational Anti-poverty Policies

The War on Poverty educational policies did do what they intended to do. The Head Start program was a major initiative of Great Society anti-poverty efforts that was established to provide disadvantaged children with experiences and resources that would enable them to compete on a more equal basis with other students when they begin their formal education. A national review of 36 studies on the long-term impact of early childhood education programs found that low-income children who participated in such programs were less likely to be held back in school or to be placed in special education classes, and were more likely to succeed in school, to graduate, and to be rated as behaving well in class and being better adjusted in school.[6] The study concluded that the typical child completing Head Start has knowledge and skills in early literacy and numeric and skills that signify a readiness to learn

4 Irwin Unger, *The Best of Intentions: The Triumph and Failure of the Great Society Under Kennedy, Johnson, and Nixon* (New York, NY: Doubleday Press, 1996), 350–60.

5 Michael L. Gillette, *Launching the War on Poverty: An Oral History* (New York, NY: Twayne Publishers, 1996), 359.

6 W. S. Barnett, "Long-Term Effects of Early Childhood Programs on Cognitive and School Outcomes." *The Future of Children* 5, no. 3 (1995): 25–50.

more in kindergarten, such as listening and comprehension skills.[7] Despite more than 30 years of investment and a proven track record in helping children and families succeed; however, Head Start is still reaching slightly less than half of the eligible preschooled-age children.[8]

Title I of the Elementary and Secondary Education Act (ESEA) of 1965, provided federal funds to school districts with a large number of low-income students. It contributed to the cognitive, social, and emotional development of poor children, and provided special services for low-achieving children to schools with low revenues. Introduced by legislation in 1965, Title I initially exhibited limited effectiveness. It provided special programs that enrolled only low-income students within a student body and often consisted of calling each student out from regular classes for only a few minutes of additional instruction per day, which were often taught by non-certified teacher's aides. The differences in expectations were evident: Measured by a common test, an A student in a high-poverty school would be a C student in a low-poverty school.[9] Programs such as ESEA and Head Start have been described as either leverage or bribes offered through federal funds, often on a matching basis, that persuade states to undertake actions they otherwise might have ignored.[10]

The ESEA has addressed national policy goals by allocating federal funds to state and local entities, the federal partner has been under pressure to demonstrate results without transgressing state and local authority.[11] The essentiality of education as a key to individual earnings and family income as well as a road to personal development has become more obvious in recent years, demands on the education system have risen precipitously, and the system has been unable to respond satisfactorily to the publics' expectations.[12] Presently, the No Child Left Behind Act, formerly ESEA, promised to close the "achievement gap" by persuading state and local education systems to establish high academic standards for all students, including disadvantaged, and requiring states to hold school systems accountable for students achieving those standards.[13]

7 N. Zill, "Head Start Program Performance Measures: Second Progress Report" (Washington DC: U.S. Department of Health and Human Services, 1998).

8 Sar A. Levitan, Garth L. Mangum, Stephen L. Mangum, and Andrew Sum, *Programs in Aid of the Poor* (Baltimore, MD: The Johns Hopkins University Press, 2003), 178.

9 Ibid., 179.

10 Ibid., 173.

11 Ibid.

12 Ibid.

13 Ibid., 174.

Higher Education Act of 1965

The aim of the Higher Education Act of 1965 was to increase the rate of college attendance and completion by low-income youth and adults by providing federal funding for college tuition in the form of grants, loans, and work-study arrangements. Grant programs included Basis Educational Opportunity Grants (Pell Grants), Supplemental Educational Opportunity Grants, and State Incentive Grants. The Pell Grant program was and still is the largest of the programs that was initially designed to provide funding for low-income students, but in 1978 the Middle-Income Assistance Act extended the reach to higher income groups.[14]

It is clear that federal education policies have transferred considerable amounts of money to low-income students, which has helped to support their attendance at postsecondary institutions. It also appears that these programs have been effective in terms of having higher participation rates among students from lower-income families to attend college and to cover a greater portion of their total education costs.[15] According to Miller and Hexter it is important to recognize that the economic burden of college costs on low-income families remains substantially high, although federal assistance has enabled more low-income students to attend relatively expensive private institutions. In conclusion, education policies and programs have allowed some to escape poverty. Because few will not escape poverty or near poverty in the future without having some form of postsecondary education or career preparation, which will be essential to earning and sustaining income.[16]

Health Care Policies

The relationship between poverty and poor health has long been recognized, and health services are considered to be an essential part of the minimum standard of living. Health insurance enables most Americans, rich and poor, to obtain and afford medical care. Private insurance is usually obtained through employment, which usually covers about three-quarters of the non-elderly population but a much smaller proportion of the poor. Only one in five poor, non-elderly Americans and one in two of the near poor are covered by private health insurance.[17] Medical care can be casually related to poverty

14 Michael Morris and John B. Williamson, *Poverty and Policy: An Analysis of Federal Intervention Efforts* (Westport, CT: Greenwood Press, 1986), 158.

15 Ibid., 159.

16 Levitan, Mangum, Mangum, and Sum, *Programs in Aid of the Poor*, 90.

17 Ibid.

in at least two major ways. First, inadequate care can result in the perpetuation of poor health or deterioration of good health, both of which can make it difficult for an individual to acquire or maintain employment.[18] Second, the expense of medical care can thrust a previously non-poor family below the poverty line.[19] Within this context, the federal health care policy has traditionally had two explicit goals such as providing the poor with greater access to medical care of acceptable quality and reducing the cost to the poor obtaining such care. Medicaid was the most important governmental program that focused on the poor's medical care. When enacted in 1965 as Title XIX of the Social Security Act, it received relatively little attention, primarily because of the highly controversial Medicare program that was established at the same time. Medicaid, therefore, represents a prime example of the covert approach to poverty policymaking.[20]

Virtually, all analysts agreed that Medicaid and Medicare have had a dramatic impact on the ability of the poor, elderly, and minorities to obtain healthcare. The evidence is clear that the poor receive much more medical care now than they did prior to the establishment of these programs. The health of the poor appears to have improved markedly in the past two decades. There have been significant declines in conditions that have traditionally been high among the poor such as infant mortality, maternal mortality, and death rates among young children. The gap between the poor and non-poor in the incidence of chronic illnesses has also been narrowed.[21] These health gains do appear to be at least partially attributable to the federal health programs that took place during the period in which major health improvements occurred.

While the successes of the federal health programs have been notable, major problems remain in providing adequate health care to the poor, which include the lack of coverage; states' reluctance to open eligibility standards for the medically needy; physician's reluctance to accept Medicaid patients; and states deciding who should receive health care. It must also be acknowledged that the increases in access to care brought about by Medicaid have by no means eliminated the two-track system that has traditionally characterized health care in America. The poor are still more likely than the non-poor to see general practitioners (rather than specialist) and to go to an outpatient

18 Morris and Williamson, *Poverty and Policy*, 102.

19 Ibid.

20 H. Helco, "The Political Foundations of Antipoverty Policy." Paper presented at the *Institute for Research on Poverty (IRP) Conference*, Madison, WI, 1984.

21 K. Davis and C. Schoen, "Health and the War on Poverty: A Ten Year Appraisal" (Washington, DC: Brookings Institute, 1978).

clinic (rather than a doctor's office). The poor also travel further and wait longer for medical care than the non-poor. Moreover, when health status is controlled, it is found that the poor use health services less frequently than the non-poor.[22] In contrast to the impressive gains that have been recorded concerning the health of the poor, significant gaps have remained between the poor and the non-poor on virtually all indicators such as infant mortality, maternal mortality, and chronic illnesses.

In summary, the Medicaid program, which has greatly increased the funding available for health-care services for the poor, has succeeded in improving the access of the poor to medical care services. However, the overall gains have not been shared by all of the poor. The poor, who are not receiving welfare, continue to lag behind, as do groups of rural residents and poor blacks. Furthermore, the poor continue to receive care from public facilities, from non-specialists, and experience longer waiting and traveling times. Karen Davis has argued that Medicaid is unevenly distributed and for those fortunate enough to be included in Medicaid, payments are minimal, but those who are not covered and live in states with very restrictive benefits have to pay rising medical costs.

The Medicare program for the elderly differs from Medicaid, whereas it is a federal program with uniform benefits covering elderly persons of all income groups. Medicare has assured that those covered by the program receive adequate medical care, but it has been less successful in removing the financial burden of medical care bills. For some elderly with large medical bills, Medicare has undoubtedly been a major source of relief from the burden of excessive bills. However, the evidence indicates that many elderly persons continue to devote large shares of their meager incomes to medical care.[23] The programs of the last decade have not eliminated the financial hardship of medical bills on low-income families. Despite the tremendous flow of public expenditures into medical care of low-income families, the poor and the elderly continue to devote high fractions of income to medical care bills.[24] Medicaid does not cover all of the poor because of eligibility restrictions stemming from its attachment to the welfare system. Many elderly continue to face high out-of-pocket costs because Medicare excludes

22 D. Altman, "Health Care For The Poor." *Annals of the American Academy of Political and Social Science* 486 (1983): 103–121.

23 Davis Karen, "Policy Developments in Health Care." In *A Decade of Federal Antipoverty Programs: Achievements, Failures, and Lessons*. Edited by Robert H. Haveman (New York, NY: Academic Press, 1977), 213.

24 Ibid., 230.

essential medical care services and requires the elderly to contribute unlimited amounts toward their bills.[25]

Public Housing

The unrelenting housing discrimination against blacks severely limited their residential choices as well as impaired their welfare in every aspect of urban living.[26] It was not a coincidence that the special housing programs, laws and/or regulations had no intentions on improving the housing conditions of the low-income black population.

Given that, the passage of the Housing Act of 1937, low-cost housing for the poor has been a national objective, but by the time the Department of Housing and Development (HUD) was created in 1965, the "goal of a decent home and a suitable living environment for every American family" (as stated in the Housing Act of 1949) had become an impossible dream for many.

During the 1960s there was an increase in the number of housing programs developed for low-income populations, which included the Housing Act of 1965, Model Cities 1966, Douglas Commission 1967, Kaiser Commission, and Housing and Urban Development Act of 1968. The structural problems of those former housing subsidy programs have resulted in inequality, discrimination, and ineffectiveness. Studies on housing policies documented that the housing market discrimination that blacks encountered was pervasive. Interventions in the housing market by the federal government did not open non-segregated housing to racial minorities, did not reduce the amount of money that black households would pay for poor-quality housing and neighborhoods, and did not assist the majority of the low-income population in need of adequate housing.[27]

In 1965, HUD's mission was to encourage economic growth in and around cities, to provide mortgage assistance to veterans and first-time homeowners, and to build housing for the urban poor. The Federal Housing Administration triggered suburban expansion by recruiting developers and homebuyers to a relatively new, untested market.[28] Since its inception, HUD has had a straightforward method: to develop good relations with mayors

25 Ibid.

26 Phyllis A. Wallace, "Policy Development in Employment and Housing." In *A Decade of Federal Antipoverty Programs: Achievements, Failures, and Lessons.* Edited by Robert H. Haveman (New York, NY: Academic Press, 1977), 349.

27 Ibid., 355.

28 Sudhir Venkatesh, "To Fight Poverty, Tear Down HUD," *The New York Times*, July 25, 2008. www.NYTimes.com.

and local real estate leaders, then award grants and underwrite loans that affirmed local development priorities.[29] As a result of HUD's myopic focus on gentrifying urban cores throughout the last four decades, the urban landscape has changed from discrete, independent cities to vast, interdependent regions where people and goods move freely, and cities have no choice but to collaborate on decisions over land use and economic development.[30]

Housing Opportunities for People Everywhere (HOPE VI) was one of the programs launched in 1992 that represented a dramatic turning point in public housing policy and redevelopment efforts in the nation's history.[31] HOPE VI replaced severely distressed public housing projects that were occupied exclusively by poor families. It redesigned projects into mixed-income housing, which provided housing vouchers to permit some of the original residents to rent apartments in the private market. As a result, HOPE VI has helped to transform the Department of Housing and Urban Development's (HUD) approach to housing assistance for the poor.[32] Congress enacted the HOPE VI program, which combined grants for physical revitalization with funding for management improvements and supportive services to promote resident self-sufficiency. Initially, housing authorities were allowed to propose plans covering up to 500 units with grant awards of up to $50 million. The program's stated objectives were as follows: to improve the living environment for residents of severely distressed public housing through the demolition, rehabilitation, reconfiguration, or replacement of obsolete projects (or portions thereof); to revitalize sites on which such public housing projects are located and contribute to the improvement of the surrounding neighborhoods; to provide housing that will avoid or decrease the concentration of very low-income families; and to build sustainable communities.[33]

In *A Decade of HOPE VI: Research Findings and Policy Challenges*, Susan J. Popkin argued that HOPE VI has not been "one program" with a clear set of consistent and unwavering goals, it has evolved in legislation, regulation, implementation, and practice, which has been shaped more through implementation than by enactment. According to Popkin, HOPE VI was initially conceived as a redevelopment and community-building program that has evolved over

29 Ibid.

30 Ibid.

31 Susan J. Popkin, Bruce Katz, Mary K. Cunningham, Karen D. Brown, Jeremy Gustafson, and Margery A. Turner, "A Decade of HOPE VI: Research Findings and Policy Challenges" (Washington, DC: The Urban Institute, 2004), 1.

32 Ibid.

33 United States Housing Act of 1937, Section 24 as amended by Section 535 of the Quality Housing and Work Responsibility Act of 1998 (P.L. 105-276).

time into an ambitious effort to build economically integrated communities that gave existing residents choices in the private housing market.

HUD ignored studies stating that former public housing residents would have difficulty finding rental housing in outlying neighborhoods and HUD did not provide assistance for inner-ring suburbs with high rates of foreclosures; HUD resisted calls to slow down public housing demolition and to move the poor to areas of high job growth; and made no effort to ascertain needs and resources on a regional scale, HUD has ended up eliminating poverty in one place while creating distressed, low-income communities in others.[34] According to Professor Sudhir Venkatesh, of Columbia University, if HUD had developed a broader vision, one that tied together inner city and suburbs, it could have created policies to help both areas adjust to the modern urban landscape.

Conclusion

In "Will the War on Poverty Change America?" S. M. Miller and Martin Rein concluded that the primary influence of the war on poverty was to improve the opportunities of the poor by changing them rather than changing the institutions that shaped them. They argued that the rehabilitative programs in work training assumed that if the poor were trained, motivated, and re-motivated, they would have been able to increase their chances in the main economy. The employing institutions were not major targets of change, so they did nothing to insure employment of the poor. The government's refusal to face social change has been revealed in its willingness to continuously give funds to institutions that have failed time and again with the poor.[35] It was not the responsibility of the individual to satisfy the needs of the programs, but the programs' responsibility to satisfy the individual and programs have failed to satisfy the needs of individuals.

The Economic Opportunity Act was identified with the Great Society's commitment to lessen or eliminate poverty. Its aim was not only to eliminate poverty but also to restructure society by giving the poor a chance to design and administer anti-poverty programs.[36] However, poverty has not been eliminated, society has not been restructured, and clearly the war on

---

34 Venkatesh, "To Fight Poverty, Tear Down HUD."

35 S. M. Miller and Martin Rein, "Will the War on Poverty Change America." In *How We Lost the War on Poverty*. Edited by Marc Pilisuk and Phyllis Pilisuk (New Brunswick, NJ: Transaction Books, 1973), 202.

36 Sar A. Levitan, Preface to *The Great Society's Poor Law* (Baltimore, MD: John Hopkins Press, 1969), ix.

poverty died prematurely. Expenditures under the Economic Opportunity Act accounted for only a small part of the total assistance to the poor, and in 1969, appropriations of nearly 2 billion under the Economic Opportunity Act's provisions constituted only 8 percent of all federal anti-poverty dollars.[37]

Although the War on Poverty fell short of its promise such as eliminating, and lessening poverty, does not mean that it was a complete failure, it did affect the lives of millions of impoverished Americans. The Great Society anti-poverty policies, which are still in existence, were the first to include African Americans on the policy agenda. The anti-poverty policies were planned on the assumption that self-help was the most effective way to escape poverty, which is the reason why poverty is so persistent among African Americans. Although African Americans were placed in training and educational programs to improve their economic and social conditions, many remained poor and could not obtain jobs in the competitive labor market.

The Great Society legislation was the most important piece of legislation concerning equal opportunity ever passed by Congress, it was also considered to be the backbone that eliminated discrimination throughout American society and guaranteed people of color an equal opportunity. The anti-poverty programs did improve the conditions for African Americans, it gave them chance at having medical care, affordable housing, and educational training that would lead to full-time employment and income. Unfortunately, the Great Society was seen as a failure; most asserted that its policies had fostered dependence on the state, nurtured irresponsible behavior, and led to the overall deterioration of the inner-city communities.

Conservatives contend that the federal government's efforts to help the poor during the 1960s were almost unlimited and that despite these efforts, poverty increased and became more severe because the well-meaning government programs backfired, while leaving their intended beneficiaries worse off.[38] In contrast, the funding of social programs during the 1960s remained modest in relation to the enormity of the problem and the war in Vietnam diminished the funds available for the War on Poverty.[39] Nonetheless, despite the limited appropriations provided, poverty declined significantly. Overall, the anti-poverty programs managed to cut the poverty rate from

---

37 Ibid.

38 Sar A. Levitan, *The Great Society's Poor Law* (Baltimore, MD: John Hopkins Press, 1969), 143.

39 Jill Quadagno, *The Color of Welfare: How Racism Undermined the War on Poverty* (New York, NY: Oxford University Press, 1994), 105, 145.

Table 4.1 Poverty rate by race, 1965–2022.

Year	*African American*	*White American*
2022	17.1	8.6
2021	19.5	8.1
2009	25.8	9.4
2000	22.5	7.4
1995	29.3	8.5
1990	31.9	8.8
1985	31.3	9.7
1980	32.5	9.1
1975	31.3	8.6
1970	33.5	9.9
1965	41.8	13.3

Source: United States Census Bureau, Current Population Survey, 1965–2022 Annual Social and Economic Supplements.

double digits in the 1960s to single digits in the early 1970s.[40] Government programs combined with economic growth had reduced poverty among Americans in general by more than half and among African Americans by nearly half.[41] The Census Bureau Historical Poverty Tables (Table 4.1) show that poverty rates actually move steadily upward immediately after the Great Society and did not begin to decline again until the 1990s. Despite this fact, some have argued that the dramatic decline was not due to the result of the Great Society but because of the growing economy.

Great Society Impact on African Americans

The Great Society programs of the 1960s, improved the lives of millions of Americans in many ways. The Food Stamp program reduced persistent hunger and malnutrition. Medicare and Medicaid improved health care dramatically for the poor and the elderly. Gains among African Americans were particularly evident. Between 1950 and 1965, before the great expansion of federal medical care and nutritional programs, the infant mortality rate of African Americans barely fell, and after the expansion of the programs, the rate of African American infant mortality declined relatively quickly.[42] The

40 U.S. Bureau of the Census, Current Population Surveys, Historical Poverty Tables. www.census.gov.

41 Ibid.

42 Linda Faye Williams, *The Constraint of Race: Legacies of White Skin Privilege in America* (University Park, PA: The Pennsylvania State University Press, 2003), 147.

housing programs lessened overcrowding and the number of people living in substandard housing; African Americans residing in overcrowded housing was reduced by more than 50 percent between 1950 and 1970.[43] Operation Head Start helped thousands of poor children prepare for school; Upward Bound prepared large number of adolescents for college; and financial assistance permitted many young people from families with low-income to gain higher education.

African Americans were key beneficiaries of many of the programs of the Great Society, because they were disproportionately represented among the ranks of the ill-housed, the poorly educated, the underemployed, and the recipients of inferior health care.[44] Great Society programs had a pronounced impact on the inner cities, heavily populated by African Americans, since almost all federally funded social services were delivered through state and local governments.[45]

The Great Society was not a total success, but it did represent a momentary break from the old immorality and corruption, which cause material and psychological effects such as a tremendous sense of hope and optimism in black communities.[46] Unfortunately, after 1968 public investments in jobs, education, and neighborhoods were diminished. The Great Society programs were short-lived, the resources and funding were not enough to produce greater change.[47] As a result, poverty remained unacceptably high. Millions of Americans still lacked health insurance. Housing remained a major problem. Hunger was still a national disgrace, and education in urban areas continued to be a disaster.[48]

43 John Schwarz, *America's Hidden Success: A Reassessment of Twenty Years of Public Policy* (New York, NY: Norton Press, 1983), 47–50.

44 Williams, *The Constraint of Race*, 150.

45 Ibid.

46 Ibid., 153.

47 Ibid.

48 Ibid., 155.

Chapter 5

CONCLUSION

The persistent poverty that exists among African Americans in the United States is a result of the unanticipated consequence of public policy that was intended to alleviate or lessen poverty, but has in fact, caused it to worsen. Federal policies have had an impact on African Americans; some policies have prevented, changed, or eradicated undesirable social conditions, while others have caused African Americans to remain deprived and disadvantaged. The outcome of public policies has had a negative effect on African Americans, contributing significantly to their persistent state of poverty, causing them to face unemployment, underemployment, and inadequate access to health care, housing, and education. However, these deep disparities did not emerge out of a vacuum, they have resulted from a set of institutional policies and practices that has collectively blocked African Americans from opportunity, support, and equality.[1] African Americans have lived with conditions filled with inequality, racism, and discrimination that continue to suffer from the circumstances forced upon them through the economic, political, and social structures within the American governmental system.

Federal policies have been partially responsible for creating the persistent poverty involving African Americans, given that they are implemented within the bureaucratic systems of government, which blame individuals for being poor instead of blaming the bureaucratic system. Policymakers have confused and misconstrued policies, focusing solely on the individual's characteristics as the main cause of poverty. African Americans did not cause their own poverty problems; the structural failings at the economic, political, and social levels are responsible for perpetuating poverty, causing African Americans to have limited opportunities and resources to achieve equality, income, and wealth.

---

1 Daniel R. Meyer and Geoffrey L. Wallace, "Poverty Levels and Trends in Comparative Perspectives." In *Changing Poverty, Changing Policies.* Edited by Maria Cancian and Sheldon Danziger (New York, NY: Russell Sage Foundation, 2009), 20.

The War on Poverty Great Society legislation was an ambitious governmental effort used to address the problem of persistent poverty in the United States. President Lyndon B. Johnson tried to rectify the inequities that existed in the United States among African Americans, by transforming the nation's social policy. Lyndon B. Johnson's Great Society legislation was notable, but it did not lessen or eliminate poverty among African Americans. Although President Lyndon B. Johnson's Great Society Legislation anti-poverty policies and programs made an impact on the lives of many African Americans during the 1960s, many African Americans continued to live in poverty, suffering from poor health, health care, education, and poor housing. Johnson's War on Poverty policies and programs were ill-advised, short-lived, underfunded, injudicious, and based on false assumptions and preconceived notions that have remained permanent to date. Policymakers blamed the victim and believed that individuals had a problem and needed to be "fixed," and not the governmental system.

Since 1965, the U.S. Census Bureau has reported that poverty rates have been higher among African Americans than white Americans. In the United States, the poverty rates above 20 percent consist of African Americans, people living in a family whose head of household does not have a job, a high school diploma, or a college degree.[2] Within the United States, those with low wages or no wages are at a very high risk of poverty because public policies and social welfare programs that add to low wages have not been generous enough to reduce or eradicate poverty.[3] One of the main reasons for the failure of the anti-poverty programs and policies is the structural problems within the system. Another reason for the failure within the system was its inopportune involvement in the liberal-conservative ideological debate on lessening or eliminating poverty among African Americans. The attitudes of policymakers have perpetuated the persistent poverty that exists among African Americans, through the use and implementation of failed governmental policies. Policies have been implemented on the basis of fixed preconceived notions about the poor, and policymakers' ideologies have misguided people, groups, and communities down the wrong path, by selecting the same goals, same objectives, and choosing the same means to eliminate poverty, which has not been a success. The anti-poverty policies and programs that were designed to alleviate poverty problems have failed the populations that were most in need, particularly poor African Americans.

2 Ibid., 56–57.

3 Ibid., 57.

Welfare was never intended to strengthen, unify, or take families above the poverty line, it was used to supplement low earnings or no earnings, but it has not provided an adequate amount of income to lessen or eliminate poverty. Welfare reform was designed with time limits, which discontinued recipients' benefits, forcing them into low-wage labor that will not meet their families' basic needs. In *Race and Recession: How Inequality Rigged the Economy and How to Change the Rules*, Seth Wessler argued that the social support system was not sufficient, and as a result, welfare reform has regulated poor individuals into low-wage work; restricting their access to income-support programs, which have left many poor families with no support at all, pushing them into poverty.[4] Low-wage work did not move recipients above the poverty line, it did not pay a livable wage, and its effects have caused persistent poverty among African Americans. Welfare reform has failed to help recipients obtain an education, get affordable housing, or adequate access to health care, eventually forcing individuals into low-wage labor and poverty.[5] Conservatives and liberals have argued that welfare was a failed policy reliant on an inefficient bureaucracy that entrenched families into poverty. Both conservatives and liberals assumed that welfare reform would make families independent; and make parents work harder to lift their families out of poverty. Ironically, Aid to Families with Dependent Children (AFDC) has succeeded better than Temporary Assistance to Needy Families (TANF) at achieving those goals.[6]

The federal government played an active and deliberate role in concentrating poverty in racially segregated neighborhoods located far from amenities, shopping, and services. Public housing and residential segregation have caused African Americans to remain socially and economically deprived within neighborhoods. The location of public housing has increased African Americans obstacles to independence and economic advancement. Positioning African Americans in old, deteriorating buildings has allowed them to suffer from a number of problems such as high concentrations of poverty, joblessness, poor school systems, worse health outcomes, lack of economic opportunities, negative role models, hopelessness, and social isolation.[7] Various structures and institutions aggravated by public policy have kept poor

4 Seath Wessler, "Race and Recession: How Inequality Rigged the Economy and How to Change the Rules." Applied Research Center. Advancing Racial Justice Through Research, Advocacy and Journalism, May 2009. www.arc.org.

5 Ibid., 15.

6 Ibid., 29.

7 Michael Katz, *Reframing the Underclass Debate: Views from History* (Princeton, NJ: Princeton University Press, 1993), 452.

African Americans from moving up and have influenced their stagnation.[8] Housing policies have awarded white communities with better education, better health, greater access to jobs and more reliable transportation, while leaving African Americans and their communities behind and deprived.[9]

The structural and historical cumulative effects of past housing policies, discrimination, and residential segregation have hindered African Americans, forcing them into poverty, preventing them from acquiring equity and access to credit that will increase wealth. The fragmented history and purpose of housing policies in the United States have demonstrated the lack of importance in recognizing and mitigating the unintended consequences of public policy choices. The structural problems of former housing subsidy programs have resulted in inequality, discrimination, and ineffectiveness. Public housing policy programs have failed to address the needs of poor African Americans, perpetuating poverty, limiting residential choices, and deteriorating their well-being, while having no intentions to improve their housing conditions.

The War on Poverty educational policies accomplished their goals partially. The Head Start program's guiding philosophy was to invest now, and benefit later. It was based on the belief that high-quality early childhood care, education, and family services would promote success, and would pay off with a multitude of benefits, to children, their families, and society as a whole. Furthermore, research has indicated that most low-income children who have attended Head Start programs were less likely to be held back in school or to be placed in special education classes, and were more likely to succeed in school, to graduate, and to be rated as behaving well in class and being better adjusted for school.[10] The Head Start program was slightly different from other educational programs because it targeted preschool-aged children and their families, assuming that early intervention might break the cycle of poverty; it provided comprehensive school readiness that enhanced a child's physical, social, emotional, and cognitive development, which was based on the belief that high-quality early childhood care, education, and family services would promote success and pay off with a multitude of benefits, to children, their families, and society as a whole. The Head Start program was

8 Rosie Tighe, "Housing Policy and the Underclass Debate: Policy Choices and Implications (1900-1970)." *Journal of Public Affairs* 18 (Spring 2006): 53.

9 Katz, *Reframing the Underclass Debate*, 452.

10 W. S. Barnett, "Long-Term Effects of Early Childhood Programs on Cognitive and School Outcomes." *The Future of Children* 5, no. 3 (1995): 25–50.

underfunded and did not reach all of the eligible preschool-aged children in the United States.[11]

Title I of the Elementary and Secondary Education Act (ESEA) of 1965, provided federal funds to school districts with a large number of low-income students. It contributed to the cognitive, social, and emotional development of poor children, and provided special services for low-achieving children who attended schools with low revenues. The ESEA has not proven its effectiveness on behalf of African American students; the achievement gap has not been closed. African Americans attend inadequate underfunded schools, and receive a less-than-average education. The differences in expectations have been evident and when measured by a common test, an A student attending a high-poverty school, would be a C student in a low-poverty school.[12] Although the ESEA of 1965 did provide federal funds to school districts with a large number of low-income students, it did not lessen or eliminate poverty, increase earnings, nor close the achievement gaps for African Americans in comparison to white Americans.

The Higher Education Act of 1965 has increased the rate of college attendance and completion by low-income youth and adults, due to the government providing federal funding for college tuition in the form of grants, loans, and work-study arrangements with the belief that low-income individuals will have prepared for a career to earn a sustainable income, and contribute to society.[13] As a consequence of the structural problems and failures within the system, African Americans with college degrees make less than equally educated whites.[14] According to the U.S. Census Bureau data released in April 2009, African Americans, on average make less than whites, regardless of their educational level.[15] In other words, highly educated employees of color still take home smaller paychecks than comparably educated white people.[16] This is a direct result of the structural institutionalized racism that exists and maintains a racial division of labor, dramatically reducing the earnings of African Americans, perpetuating their persistent state of poverty.[17]

---

11 Sar A. Levitan, Garth L. Mangum, Stephen L. Mangum, and Andrew Sum, *Programs in Aid of the Poor* (Baltimore, MD: The Johns Hopkins University Press, 2003), 178.

12 Ibid., 179.

13 Ibid., 90.

14 Current Population Survey, Bureau of Labor Statistics, 2009.

15 Education Attainment in the U.S., 2008. www.census.gov/population/www/socdemo/edu-attn.htlm.

16 Wessler, "Race and Recession," 15.

17 Ibid.

Medicare and Medicaid enacted under the Great Society legislation affected African Americans, in which they were granted access to medical care and health coverage. However, the poor had little access to medical treatment until they were in critical condition, while wealthier Americans had access to the best care. Although the federal government took full responsibility for funding health care, providing Medicare to the elderly and Medicaid to the poor, disparities in access, coverage, and care still persist. Even though Medicare has kept the health cost down for elderly individuals, the amount of coinsurance and deductibles placed on the low-income elderly is considerably high and steadily growing.[18] Regardless of federal funding for Medicare, the rising health-care cost, could eventually wipe out a major portion of the elderly individual's income, leaving them in poverty.

Medicaid provides health coverage to many of the poor, but by no means to all of the poor, and since state governments are responsible for the majority of the funding for Medicaid, it has created disparities within the system such as unequal access to medical care, health coverage, and services. Medicaid seems to have been helpful in improving the access of the poor to medical care, but poor African Americans remain stagnant and have not participated in mainstream medicine of comparable quality, convenience, or style that have been received by non-poor, whites. Poor African Americans and Hispanics continue to receive care in crowded dreary clinics, experiencing longer wait times, few amenities, and traveling far away to receive care.[19]

The majority of anti-poverty policies and programs were based on the notion that a culture of poverty does exist, which has deliberately guided policies in a specific direction. A Culture of Poverty does not exist and it has not caused African Americans to remain persistently poor. Policymakers who designed policies that blame the poor for their own problems, consequently relinquished the governmental institutions from their social duties, creating systematic failures within the structure of government. Therefore, once poverty is viewed as the responsibility of the poor and not the government, their culture, not social injustice, causes and perpetuates poverty among African Americans. The political, economic, and social structures of government are flawed and it is the primary reason why African Americans have remained poor and underprivileged in the United States, not because of a culture of poverty. Reconceptualizing poverty and blaming the system

---

18 Levitan, Mangum, Mangum, and Sum, *Programs in Aid of the Poor*, 91.

19 Karen Davis, "A Decade of Policy Developments in Providing Health Care for Low-Income Families." In *A Decade of Federal Antipoverty Programs: Achievements, Failures, and Lessons.* Edited by Robert H. Haveman (New York, NY: Academic Press, 1977), 204.

for its malfunctions will remove the blame from the individual, creating a paradigm shift that will offer new policies designed to lessen or eliminate poverty. Reconceptualizing poverty will allow reevaluation of the political and economic systems of government, which have produced public policies and programs that have continuously kept African Americans in persistent poverty.[20] The disappointment and failure of policies created within the political, economic, and social systems developed to lessen or eliminate poverty have created negative attitudes and behaviors within the African American culture, because government institutions have continuously oppressed them at all levels of society.

Poverty is a deep, structural problem that has disadvantaged African Americans in the United States. The past structural failures within the system must be challenged, reevaluated, and resolved. Policymakers will have to introduce a new highly developed policy agenda that will clearly challenge the problem of persistent poverty that exists among African Americans in the United States. Moving forward, the U.S. government must address and correct its structural flaws, first creating policies to confront the cumulative and compounding causes of racial inequality. Persistent, recurring racial disparities and barriers to possibilities for African Americans have been ignored, because the governmental system has blamed the individual for their own poverty problems, and mainly focused on how to "fix" the poor, while not acknowledging the flaws within the governmental system.

The following recommendations for the future will promote change within the U.S. governmental institutions. The recommendations will correct and challenge the old misdirected policies and programs that were designed to minimize or eliminate poverty. Future recommendations will provide the federal government with new prescriptions, frameworks, and guidelines on reconceptualizing poverty, which will result in a paradigm shift.

Policy Recommendations:

I. Develop an **Overarching Policymaking Framework**

A policymaking framework would provide a mechanism that will systematically address racial inequities during the policymaking process.[21] The framework would expand the use of Racial Equity Impact Training

20 Leonard Beeghley, *Living Poorly In America* (New York, NY: Praeger Publishers, 1983), 134.

21 Wessler, "Race and Recession," 47.

& Assessments for public planning and policymaking, to make certain that racial inequality will be prevented prior to the adoption and of new policies and practices.

II. Provide **Comprehensive Universal Healthcare**

Reforming healthcare to meet the needs of everyone in the United States will eliminate the disparities that exist in health and access to health care and medical services. Congress should enact healthcare reform legislation that would guarantee quality, affordable healthcare to all people living in the United States, without exception.[22] Reform is needed to ensure that every citizen has access to quality and affordable health care.

III. **Reinforce Policies to Reduce Poverty and Inequality**

Enforce Anti-Discrimination Laws to ensure that all people are provided an equal opportunity, fair treatment, and are not discriminated against on the basis of race. Promoting more policies that would provide additional income to support measures, creating strategies that will encourage asset building, and credit counseling. Reinforcing policies to eliminate poverty and inequality must become a national commitment of the federal government. These policies will begin to address the harsh inequalities that exist among African Americans through the use of federal policies.

IV. **Make Full Employment a Priority and Commitment of the Federal Government**

Economic policies must be aimed at creating full employment that will provide an adequate income.[23] The government must commit to reforming policies that will create jobs, achieve full employment for African Americans, and acknowledge the failures of past and current

---

22 Ibid.

23 Ivory A. Toldson, and Elsie L. Scott, "Poverty, Race and Policy: Strategic Advancement of a Poverty Reduction Agenda" (Washington, DC: Congressional Black Caucus Foundation, 2006), 5.

economic policies.[24] This policy will reduce poverty rates among African Americans, making certain that full employment will translate into improved economic well-being. States will have to commit to helping those that face serious obstacles entering into the labor market. New policies will expand opportunities for low-wage workers, which should consist of; higher-quality jobs, higher-paying jobs, providing benefits such as sick leave, vacation time, and health care along with adequate flexibility to meet family needs.[25] This initiative will help the underemployed groups to get in or back into the workforce.

V. **Increase Minimum Wage**

Raising minimum wage to a livable wage will help low- to moderate-income families to support their families. Increasing minimum wage will help to keep low-wage workers and their families out of poverty. Increasing social welfare benefits will strengthen the social safety net. Temporary Assistance for Needy Families (TANF) time limits within the states should be suspended, until jobs are created that will provide sustainable income. Strengthen those recipients' access that is leaving (TANF) to work supports, such as Food Stamps, Medicaid, child-care, and child support.

VI. **Increase Housing Assistance**

A major focus of housing policy reform should be to develop affordable and adequate housing for the poor. The lack of affordable housing, discrimination, and residential segregation is the leading cause of poverty problems among African Americans, residing in public or unaffordable housing. Research has demonstrated that housing assistance in the form of vouchers, have been more cost-effective than housing assistance in the form of new construction, and those who receive vouchers typically live in better neighborhoods than recipients living in public housing projects.[26] Although vouchers have provided residents with a choice in

---

24 Ibid., 10.

25 Steve Savner, Julie Strawn, and Mark Greenberg, "TANF Reauthorization: Opportunities to Reduce Poverty by Improving Employment Outcomes." *Center for Law and Social Policy*, 2002. http://www.clasp.org/admin/site/publications_archive/files/0075.pdf.

26 Toldson and Scott, "Poverty, Race and Policy," 16.

Table 5.1 Poverty rate by race, 1965–2022.

Year	*African Americans*	*White Americans*
2022	17.1	8.6
2021	19.5	8.1
2009	25.8	9.4
2000	22.5	7.4
1995	29.3	8.5
1990	31.9	8.8
1985	31.3	9.7
1980	32.5	9.1
1975	31.3	8.6
1970	33.5	9.9
1965	41.8	13.3

Source: United States Census Bureau, Current Population Survey, 1965–2022 Annual Social and Economic Supplements.

selecting their units rather than being obligated to reside in a specific unit in a particular part of town, it has not solved the housing problems of the poor. The poor cannot afford to live in mixed-use income communities; therefore, new housing policies must create affordable housing and vouchers programs to benefit those that are in need.

Summary

The Great Society anti-poverty policies and programs were flawed, brief, insufficient, and unable to produce greater change for African Americans.[27] As a result, poverty has remained unacceptably high among African Americans. Millions of African Americans still lack health insurance. Unaffordable, decent rental housing has remained a major problem. Hunger is still a national disgrace, and education in urban areas has continued to be a disaster.[28] The Census Bureau Historical Poverty Tables show that since 1965 poverty rates among African Americans have decreased, but have also remained significantly higher when compared to white Americans (Table 5.1).

Regardless of the vast amount of public spending on health care for low-income, poor, and elderly individuals and families, they will continuously have

27 Linda Faye Williams, *The Constraint of Race: Legacies of White Skin Privilege in America* (University Park, PA: The Pennsylvania State University Press, 2003), 153.
28 Ibid., 155.

to devote a high portion of their income on medical care bills and services.[29] Although the enactment of Medicare and Medicaid has allowed African Americans access to medical care, a higher proportion of African Americans continuously lack coverage when compared to white Americans. The U.S. Bureau reports that in 2009, (21.0) percent of African Americans were uninsured, compared to (13.2) of whites that were not covered. The percentage of people covered by government health insurance programs increased to (29.0) percent in 2009 from (27.8) percent in 2007.[30] The percentage and number of people covered by Medicaid increased to (14.3) percent in 2009, from (13.2) percent in 2007; (27.1) percent were African Americans, and (9.8) were white Americans. The percentage and number of people covered by Medicare in 2009 (14.3), which was not statistically different from 2008, (11.9) are African Americans, and (15.4) are whites.[31]

President Lyndon B. Johnson assumed that education and training programs would transform many people's lives and lead to a higher income for individuals and their families, preventing poverty. In addition, education policies and training programs have allowed some to escape poverty, but the majority of African Americans constantly lag behind whites in educational attainment. The U.S. Census Bureau reports that in 2008, in terms of college education, 33 percent of Whites, and 20 percent of Blacks had obtained at least a bachelor's degree. Although the attainment rates of bachelor degrees for all racial/ethnic groups have increased over the past 12 years, educational achievement gaps are not narrowing, they have been widening.[32] The figures below demonstrate that between 1996 and 2008, the percentage of adults who had obtained at least a bachelor's degree increased, but African Americans percentage points remained the lowest: percentage points for Asians/Pacific Islanders increased by 10, percentage points for Whites by 7, and percentage points for Blacks by 6 (Figure 5.1).[33]

The housing policies and subsidy programs negatively impacted African Americans, resulting in inequality, discrimination, and ineffectiveness. African Americans with low income, or near low income are less likely to own their home, have to live in substandard housing, with less comfortable

29 Davis, "Policy Developments in Health Care," 230.

30 United States Census Bureau. "Health Insurance Coverage Status and Type of Coverage - All Persons by Sex, Race and Hispanic Origin 1999 to 2009." Health Insurance Historical Tables. www.census.gov.

31 Ibid.

32 National Center For Education Statistics. U.S. Department of Education Institute of Education Sciences. http://nces.ed.gov/pubs2010/2010015/figures/figure_27.asp.

33 Ibid.

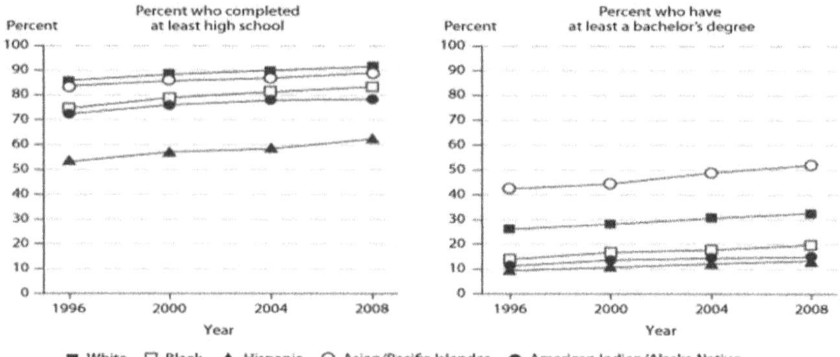

Figure 5.1 Percentage of adults ages 25 and over who completed at least high school and the percentage who have at least a bachelor's degree, by race/ethnicity: Selected years, 1996–2008. Source: U.S. Department of Commerce, Census Bureau, Current Population Survey (CPS), Annual Demographic Supplement, 1996, 2000, 2004, and Annual Social and Economic Supplement, 2008.

living conditions, and constantly face cost burdens. Housing policies have not permitted the poor to live in decent affordable housing; they have been forced to live in inferior housing (smaller, crowded, and saddled with physical problems).[34] Housing policies created on the origin of faulty ideologies are responsible for the ineffectiveness of policies that were expected to eliminate or lessen poverty among African Americans, which has in fact caused it to worsen.

Due to the flawed conceptualizations of poverty among African Americans, policymakers have implemented ineffective, erroneous policies to eradicate poverty. The inability of President Lyndon B. Johnson's Great Society Legislation to reduce or eliminate poverty among African Americans was severely constrained, because it was based on the preconceived notions or ideologies that blamed the individual for his or her poverty problems, while failing to recognize or re-examine the failure of governmental structure/system.

34 United States Census Bureau. "Statistical Brief. "Housing of Lower-Income Households." http://www.census.gov/apsd/www/statbrief/sb94_18.pdf.

REFERENCES

Allard, Scott W. "Place, Race, and Access to the Safety Net." In *The Colors of Poverty Why Racial and Ethnic Disparities Persist*. Edited by Ann Chih Lin and David R. Harris (New York, NY: Russell Sage Foundation, 2008).

Altman, D. "Health Care For The Poor." *Annals of the American Academy of Political and Social Science* 486 (1983): 103–121.

Asen, R. *Visions of Poverty: Welfare Policy and Political Imagination* (East Lansing, MI: Michigan State University Press, 2002).

Banfield, Edward C. *The Unheavenly City Revisited* (Prospect Heights, IL: Waveland Press, 1990).

Barnett, W. S. "Long-Term Effects of Early Childhood Programs on Cognitive and School Outcomes." *The Future of Children* 5, no. 3 (1995): 25–50.

Beeghley, Leonard. *Living Poorly In America* (New York, NY: Praeger Publishers, 1983).

Bradshaw, Ted K. "Complex Community Development Projects: Collaboration, Comprehensive Programs and Community Coalitions in Complex Society." *Community Development Journal* 35, no. 2 (2001): 133–145.

Bradshaw, Ted K. "Theories of Poverty and Anti-Poverty Programs in Community Development." Rural Poverty Research Center (2005). www.rprconline.org.

Brown, Michael K. "Ghettos, Fiscal Federalism, and Welfare Reform." In *Race and the Politics of Welfare Reform*. Edited by Sanford F. Schram, Joe Soss, and Richard C. Fording (Ann Arbor, MI: The University of Michigan Press, 2003).

Burton, Emory C. *The Poverty Debate: Politics and the Poor in America* (New York, NY: Greenwood Press, 1999).

Califano, Joseph. "What was Really Great about the Great Society?" *The Washington Monthly Online*. http://www.washingtonmonthly.com.

Cancian, Maria and Danziger, Sheldon. *Changing Poverty and Changing Policies* (New York, NY: Russell Sage Foundation, 2009).

Carballo, Manuel and Bane, Mary Jo. *The State and the Poor in the 1980s* (Westport, CT: Auburn Publishing, 1984).

Corcoran, Mary. "Mobility, Persistence, and the Consequences of Poverty for Children: Child and Adult Outcomes." In *Understanding Poverty*. Edited by Sheldon H. Danziger and Robert H. Haveman (New York, NY: Russell Sage Foundation, 2009).

Corcoran, Mary. "Rags to Rags: Poverty and Mobility in the United States." *Annual Review of Sociology* 21 (1995): 245.

Danziger, Sheldon H. and Haveman, Robert H.. Introduction to *Understanding Poverty* (New York, NY: Russell Sage Foundation, 2001).

Davis, Karen. "A Decade of Policy Developments in Providing Health Care for Low-Income Families." In *A Decade of Federal Antipoverty Programs: Achievements, Failures, and Lessons.* Edited by Robert H. Haveman (New York, NY: Academic Press, 1977).

Davis, Karen and Schoen, C. "Health and the War on Poverty: A Ten Year Appraisal" (Washington, DC: Brookings Institute, 1978).

De Leeuw, Michael B., Whyte, Megan K., Ho, Dale, Meza, Catherine, and Karteron, Alexis. "Residential Segregation And Housing Discrimination in the United States: Violations of the International Convention on the Elimination of All Forms of Racial Discrimination." Executive Summary (2007).

DeNavas-Walt, Carmen, Proctor, Bernadette D., and Smith, Jessica C. "United States Census Bureau. Current Population Reports," 60–235. www.uscensusbureau.com.

Dubois, W. E. B. *Black Reconstruction in America, 1860-1880* (New York, NY: Athenaeum Press, 1985). (Originally Published in 1935).

Duncan, Greg J. *Years of Poverty, Years of Plenty* (Ann Arbor, MI: Institute for Social Research, University of Michigan Press, 1984).

Ellwood, David T. "Understanding Dependency: Choices, Confidence, or Culture" (Washington, DC: U.S. Dept. of Health and Human Services, OS, ASPE, and Income Security Policy/Research, 1987).

Gans, Herbert J. "The Uses of Poverty: The Poor Pay All." *Social Policy* (July/August 1971).

Gilder, George. *Wealth and Poverty* (New York, NY: Bantam Books, 1982).

Gillette, Michael L. *Launching The War On Poverty: An Oral History* (New York, NY: Twayne Publishers, 1996).

Goering, John M. *Housing Desegregation and Federal Policy* (Chapel Hill, NC: University of North Carolina Press, 1986).

Goldberg, Gertrude Schaffner and Collins, Shelia D. *Washington' New Poor Law: Welfare Reform and the Roads Not Taken 1935 – Present* (New York, NY: Apex Press, 2000).

Goldsmith, William W. and Blakely, Edward J. *Separate Societies: Poverty and Inequality in U.S. Cities* (Philadelphia, PA: Temple University Press, 1992).

Halloran, Daniel F. "Progress Against Poverty: The Governmental Approach." *Public Administration Review* 28, no. 3 (1968): 209.

Harrington, Michael. *The Other America* (Baltimore, MD: Penguin Books, 1971).

Heiser, Janine. "Lyndon B. Johnson's Power Prospects Strategy: The Case of the War on Poverty." Oberlin College. www.thepresidency.org/storage/documents/Calkins/Heiser.

Helco, H. "The Political Foundations of Antipoverty Policy." Paper presented at the *Institute for Research on Poverty (IRP) Conference*, Madison, WI, 1984.

Hinton, Wayne K. Foreword to Ropers, Richard H. In *Persistent Poverty: The American Dream Turned Nightmare* (New York, NY: Insight Books, Plenum Press, 1991).

Hoffman, Alexander von. "High Ambitions: The Past and Future of American Low-Income Housing Policy." *Housing Policy Debate* 7, Issue 3 (1996): 423–446.

Hyde, Henry J. "Morals, Markets and Freedoms." *National Review* 42, no. 21 (November 1990): 52–54.

Initial Report of the United States of America to the United Nations Committee on the Elimination of Racial Discrimination, at 49, delivered to the U.N. Committee on the Elimination of Racial Discrimination (September 2000). www.ushrnetwork.org.

Jackson, Kenneth T. and Kazelton, Ira. "When Affirmative Action Was White." In *Crabgrass Frontier* (2005).

Jargowsky, Paul A. *Poverty and Place: Ghettos, Barrios, and the American City* (New York, NY: Russell Sage Foundation, 1997).

Jencks, Christopher and Patterson, Paul. *The Urban Underclass* (Washington, DC: The Brookings Institute Washington, 1991).

Katz, Michael B. *The "Underclass" Debate: Views from History* (Princeton, NJ: Princeton University Press, 1993).

Katz, Michael B. *The Undeserving Poor: From the War on Poverty to the War on Welfare* (New York, NY: Pantheon, 1989).

Kearns, Doris. *Lyndon Johnson and the American Dream* (New York, NY: Harper & Row, 1976.

Krumholtz, Norman. "The Reluctant Hand: Privatization of Public Housing in the U.S." Paper presented at the *CITY FUTURES CONFERENCE*, Chicago, July 8–10, 2004.

Kushnick, Louis and Jennings, James. *A New Introduction to Poverty: The Role of Race, Power, and Politics* (New York, NY: University Press, 1999).

Lamont, Michele and Small, Mario Luis. "How Culture Matters: Enriching Our Understanding of Poverty." In *The Colors of Poverty: Why Racial and Ethnic Disparities Persist.* Edited by Lin, Ann Chih and David R. Harris (New York, NY: The Russell Sage Foundation, 2008).

Larner, Mary B., Terman, Donna L., and Behrman, Richard E. "The Future of the Children." *Welfare to Work* 27, no. 7 (Spring 1997): 4.

Levin, Henry M. "A Decade of Policy Developments In Improving Education and Training for Low-Income Populations." In *A Decade of Federal Antipoverty Programs: Achievements, Failures, and Lessons.* Edited by Robert H. Haveman (New York, NY: Academic Press, 1977).

Levitan, Sar A. Preface to *The Great Society's Poor Law* (Baltimore, MD: Johns Hopkins Press, 1969).

Levitan, Sar A., Mangum, Garth L., Mangum, Stephen L., and Sum, Andrew. *Programs in Aid of the Poor* (Baltimore, MD: The Johns Hopkins University Press, 2003).

Lewis, Oscar. *Anthropology Essays* (New York, NY: Random House Press, 1970).

Lewis, Oscar. *La Vida: A Puerto Rican Family in the Culture of Poverty* (New York, NY: Random House Press, 1996).

Lin, Ann Chih and Harris, David R. "Why is American Poverty Still Colored in the Twenty-First Century." In *The Colors of Poverty: Why Racial and Ethnic Disparities Persist* . Edited by Ann Chih Lin and David R. Harris (New York, NY: Russell Sage Foundation, 2008), 4.

Listoken, David. "Federal Housing Policy and Preservation: Historical Evolution, Patterns, and Implications." *Housing Policy Debate* 2, Issue 2 (1991); 163–164.

Lynn, Laurence E. "Policy Developments in Income Maintenance System." In *A Decade of Federal Antipoverty Programs: Achievements, Failures, and Lessons.* Edited by Robert H. Haveman (New York, NY: Academic Press, 1977).

Magnum, Garth L. and Walsh, John. *A Decade of Manpower Development Training* (Salt Lake City, UT: Olympus Publishing Co., 1973).

Mandel, Jay R. *The Roots of Black Poverty: The Southern Plantation Economy After the Civil War* (Durham, NC: Duke University Press, 1978).

March, Michael S. "Coordination of the War on Poverty." In *Anti-Poverty Programs.* Edited by Robinson O. Everett (Dobbs Ferry, NY: Oceana Publications, Inc., 1966), 139.

Massey, Douglas S. and Denton, Nancy. *American Apartheid: Segregation and the Making of the Underclass* (Cambridge, MA: Harvard University Press, 1993).

Matusow, Allen J. *The Unraveling of America: A History of Liberalism in the 1960's* (New York, NY: Harper Torchbooks, 1984).

Mead, Lawrence M. *Beyond Entitlement: The Social Obligations of Citizenship* (New York, NY: The Free Press, 1986).

Mead, Lawrence M. *The New Politics of Poverty: The Nonworking Poor in America* (New York, NY: HarperCollins Publishers, 1992).

Merriam, S. B. *Qualitative Research and Case Study Application in Education* (San Francisco, CA: Jossey-Bass Publisher, 1998).

Meyer, Daniel R. and Wallace, Geoffrey L. "Poverty Levels and Trends in Comparative Perspectives." In *Changing Poverty, Changing Policies*. Edited by Maria Cancian and Sheldon Danziger (New York, NY: Russell Sage Foundation, 2009).

Miller, S. M. and Rein, Martin. "Will the War on Poverty Change America." In *How We Lost the War on Poverty*. Edited by Marc Pilisuk and Phyllis Pilisuk (New Brunswick, NJ: Transaction Books, 1973).

Mills, Wright C. *The Sociological Imagination* (New York, NY: Oxford University Press, Inc., 2000).

Morrill, R. L. and Wohlenberg, E. H. *The Geography of Poverty* (New York, NY: McGraw Hill, 1971).

Morris, Michael and Williamson, John B. *Poverty and Policy: An Analysis of Federal Intervention Efforts* (Westport, CT: Greenwood Press, 1986).

Moynihan, Daniel P. "The Negro Family" (Washington, DC: US Department of Labor, Office of Policy Planning and Research, 1965).

Murray, Charles. *Losing Ground: American Social Policy 1950-1980* (New York, NY: Basic Books, HarperCollins Publishers, Inc., 1984).

Murray, V. McBride, Smith, Emeli Ph., and Hill, Nancy E.. "Race, Ethnicity, and Culture in Studies of Families in Context." *Journal of Marriage and Family* 4, no. 63, (November 2001): 911–915.

O'Neil, Kenneth. *Nixon's Piano: Presidents and Racial Politics From Washington to Clinton* (New York, NY: Free Press, 1995).

Pager, Devah. "The Dynamics of Discrimination." In *The Colors of Poverty Why Racial and Ethnic Disparities Persist*. Edited by Ann Chih Lin and David R. Harris (New York, NY: The Russell Sage Foundation, 2008).

Parrott, Sharon. "Welfare Recipients Who Find Jobs: What Do We Know About Their Employment Earnings?" *Center on Budget and Policy Priorities* (November 1998). www.cbpp.org.

Quadagno, Jill. *The Color of Welfare: How Racism Undermined the War on Poverty* (New York, NY: Oxford University Press, 1994).

Rank, Mark Robert. *ONE NATION, UNDERPRIVLEDGED: Why American Poverty Affects Us All* (New York, NY: Oxford University Press, 2004).

Robson, Colin. *Real World Research: A Resource for Social Scientist and Practicioners-Researchers* (Malden, MA: Blackwell Press, 2002).

Ropers, Richard H. *Persistent Poverty: The American Dream Turned Nightmare* (New York, NY: Insight Books, Plenum Press, 1991).

Ryan, William. *Blaming the Victim* (New York, NY: Random House Press, Inc., 1972, Revised 1976).

Sawhill, Isabel V. "Senior Fellow, Economic Studies Ron Haskins, Senior Fellow, Economic Studies" (2003). http://www.brookings.edu/papers/2003/09childrenfamilies.

Schiller, Bradley R. *The Economics of Poverty and Discrimination* (Upper Saddle River, NJ: Pearson Prentice Hall, Inc., 2004).

Schram, Sanford F., Soss, Joe, and Fording, Richard. *Race and the Politics of Welfare Reform* (Ann Arbor, MI: University of Michigan Press, 2003).

Schwarz, John. *America's Hidden Success: A Reassessment of Twenty Years of Public Policy* (New York, NY: Norton Press, 1983).

Shaw, W. *The Geography of United States Poverty* (New York, NY: Garland Publishing, 1996).

Sherraden, Michael. *Assets and the Poor* (Armonk, NY: M.E. Sharpe Press, 1991).

Solomon, Rod. "Public Housing Reform and Voucher Success: Progress and Challenges." *Brookings Institute* (January 2005) (Federal Policy - 235). www.brookings.edu.

Stoll, Michael A. "Race Place and Poverty Revisited." In *The Colors of Poverty: Why Racial and Ethnic Disparities Persist.* Edited by Ann Chih Lin and David R. Harris (New York, NY: Russell Sage Foundation, 2008).

Strauss, A. and Corbin, J. *Basics of Qualitative Research: Grounded Theory Procedures and Techniques* (Newbury Park, CA: Sage Publications, Inc., 1990).

Stricker, Frank. *Why America Lost The War On Poverty – And How To Win It* (Chapel Hill, NC: The University of North Carolina Press, 2007).

Tighe, Rosie. "Housing Policy and The Underclass Debate: Policy Choices and Implications (1900–1970)." *Journal of Public Affairs* 18 (Spring 2006): 53.

Tolnay, Stewart E., Adelman, Robert M., and Crowder, Kyle D. "Race, Regional Origin, and Residence in Northern Cities at the Beginning of the Great Migration." *American Sociological Review* 67, no. 3 (June 2002): 457–458.

Unger, Irwin. *The Best of Intentions: The Triumph and Failures of the Great Society Under Kennedy, Johnson, and Nixon* (Chicago, IL: Doubleday Press, 1996).

United States Bureau of the Census, Current Population Surveys, Historical Poverty Tables. www.census.gov.

United States Census Bureau. "People in Families with Related Children by Family Structure, Age, and Sex, Iterated by Income-to-Poverty Ratio and Race." Table POV03 (2007). www.uscensusbureau.

United States Census Bureau. www.census.gov/hhe/poverty.

United States Department of Housing and Urban Development. www.hud.gov.

Vale, Lawrence J. *From the Puritans to the Projects: Public Housing and Public Neighbors* (Cambridge, MA: Harvard University Press, 2000).

Valentine, Charles A. *Culture and Poverty: Critique and Counter Proposals* (Chicago, IL: The University of Chicago Press, 1970).

Venkatesh, Sudhir. "To Fight Poverty, Tear Down HUD." *The New York Times* (July 25, 2008). www.NYtimes.com.

Wallace, Phyllis A. "Policy Development in Employment and Housing." In *A Decade of Federal Antipoverty Programs: Achievements, Failures, and Lessons.* Edited by Robert H. Haveman (New York, NY: Academic Press, 1977).

Waxman, Chaim. *Stigma of Poverty: A Critique of Poverty Theories and Policies* (New York, NY: Pergamon Press, 1983).

Williams, Linda Faye. *The Constraint of Race: Legacies of White Skin Privilege in America* (University Park, PA: The Pennsylvania State University Press, 2003).

Wilson, William Julius, *The Truly Disadvantaged: The Inner City, the Underclass, and Public Policy* (Chicago, IL: The University of Chicago Press, 1987).

Yin, Robert. *A Case Study Research: Design and Methods. Applied Social Research Methods.* 2nd ed. (Thousand Oaks, CA: Sage Publications, Inc., 2009).

Yinger, John. "Housing Discrimination and Residential Segregation." In *Understanding Poverty*. Edited by Sheldon H. Danziger and Robert H. Haveman (New York, NY: Russell Sage Foundation, 2001).

Zigler, Edward and Muenchow, Susan. *Head Start: The Inside Story of America's Most Successful Educational Experiment* (New York, NY: Basic Books, 1992).

Zill, N. "Head Start Program Performance Measures: Second Progress Report" (Washington, DC: U.S. Department of Health and Human Services, 1998).

INDEX

Milton Keynes UK
Ingram Content Group UK Ltd.
UKHW020313300924
449022UK00001B/11

9 781839 991882